浙江省社科规划课题成果(19NDJC044Y

中国"一带一路"
对外新闻话语研究

蒋国东　著

A DISCOURSE STUDY OF
"BELT AND ROAD" ENGLISH NEWS
BY CHINESE MEDIA

ZHEJIANG UNIVERSITY PRESS
浙江大学出版社

图书在版编目（CIP）数据

中国"一带一路"对外新闻话语研究 / 蒋国东著
. —杭州：浙江大学出版社，2019.11
ISBN 978-7-308-19683-3

Ⅰ.①中… Ⅱ.①蒋… Ⅲ.①中国对外政策－宣传工
作－新闻语言－研究 Ⅳ.①G210

中国版本图书馆 CIP 数据核字（2019）第 249598 号

中国"一带一路"对外新闻话语研究

蒋国东　著

责任编辑	祁　潇
责任校对	虞雪芬　宁　檬
封面设计	周　灵
出版发行	浙江大学出版社
	（杭州市天目山路 148 号　邮政编码 310007）
	（网址：http://www.zjupress.com）
排　　版	浙江时代出版服务有限公司
印　　刷	杭州良诸印刷有限公司
开　　本	880mm×1230mm　1/32
印　　张	8
字　　数	200 千
版 印 次	2019 年 11 月第 1 版　2019 年 11 月第 1 次印刷
书　　号	ISBN 978-7-308-19683-3
定　　价	35.00 元

前　言

　　2013 年,习近平主席在出访中亚和东南亚国家期间,先后提出共建"丝绸之路经济带"和"21 世纪海上丝绸之路"的倡议,为古丝绸之路赋予了新的时代内涵。自"一带一路"倡议提出以来,中国与沿线国家的合作日益加强,共同促进了沿线国家乃至世界经济的发展,因此也逐渐得到了国内外媒体的高度关注,相关的新闻报道不断增加。为了促进沿线各国人民对"一带一路"倡议相关新闻报道的了解和认同,国内外学者从不同的角度解读了有关"一带一路"的新闻报道。

　　本研究以 Martin 和 White 评价理论、亚里士多德古典修辞理论为理论基础,从中国一带一路网、*China Daily* 和 Xinhua News Agency 上选择新闻语料,以 White 的环绕轨道模型为依据划分"一带一路"新闻语篇结构,运用定量分析归纳此类新闻语篇中介入和态度话语资源的分布规律,运用定性分析阐释"一带一路"对外新闻语篇如何通过韵律话语策略来实现语篇交际功能和人际意义。

　　研究发现,第一,"一带一路"对外新闻语篇的开篇部分,新闻作者为了吸引读者兴趣,往往运用单声策略呈现新闻标题;为了展现客观中立的报道风格,用承认策略推出新闻导语,话语空间由此打开。在详述部分,新闻作者充分运用承认策略,转述不同新闻参与者的话语,尽可能真实还原新闻事件,话语空间进一步扩展。在解释部分,新闻作者运用支持策略,压缩对话空间,支持转述对象,承担转述话语的人际责任,为读者揭开新闻事件各元素间的逻辑关系、前因后果,解除读者心中的迷惑。在评论部分,新闻作者继续运用支持策略压缩对话空间,力图聚焦转述观点,影响读者对新闻事件的价值判断和评价立场,拉拢读者与自己结成评价同盟。在背景部分,新闻作者通过单声策略描述类似事件、后续影响等,关闭对话空间,用公认事实对比眼前新闻,巩固与读者的态度同盟,引导读者接受新闻作者植入语篇的评价立场。

第二,对外新闻语篇往往用判断资源开篇和详述,用鉴赏资源进行解释和提供背景,最后用情感资源展开评论。"一带一路"对外新闻语篇的开篇语步主要是对新闻人物的行为做出积极判断,是语篇核心人际意义的体现。详述语步是对开篇语步中的内容进行具体描述,所以两语步都是以判断资源为评价模式。鉴赏资源在对外新闻语篇中的分布主要集中在背景语步和解释语步。背景语步介绍新闻事件的发展过程,解释语步是展现新闻事件的前因后果,两语步旨在描述新闻事件的价值和构成以及新闻人物对该事件的反应。情感资源运用比例最高的是评论语步,该语步是对新闻事件的社会意义、情感影响等进行点评,旨在操纵读者的评价姿态。

　　第三，随着"一带一路"对外新闻语篇展开，各阶段介入策略为语篇构建的话语空间呈现出"关闭——扩展——收缩——关闭"的趋势，如此循环往复，形成伸缩有序的韵律话语模式。与此同时，态度韵律通常以主导型模式开场，奠定韵律基调，由多个评价音符形成回音，然后用增强型韵律模式，提升音阶，调高音量，最终用渗透型韵律模式，将评价态度融入语篇尾声。

　　第四，判断资源主要通过主导型态度韵律实现人品说服策略，鉴赏资源主要通过增强型态度韵律实现逻辑说服策略，情感资源主要通过渗透型态度韵律实现情感说服策略。判断是按照伦理、道德及法律对人的品行做出的评价。在对外新闻语篇中，新闻作者用表达判断意义的词汇构建主导型态度韵律来陈述其对某行为或人品的判断，表现新闻当事人的人品，赢得读者信任，"以德服人"，实现人品说服策略。鉴赏是对事件、事物和现象的评价。鉴赏资源通过增强型态度韵律体现新闻记者对新闻事件的反应以及对该事件的构成和价值做出评价，以引导读者去考量新闻事件本身的逻辑，"以理服人"，实现逻辑说服策略。情感资源实现情感说服目的，这是因为新闻语篇或多或少都添加了新闻作者和新闻人物的感情色彩，通过语篇中的情感资源建立渗透型态度韵律，感染读者情感，"以情动人"，促使读者接受语篇立场和观点，体现情感说服策略。

　　第五，在"一带一路"对外新闻语篇中，介入策略和话语空间都受到该语类结构与语域特征的影响,而归根到底,是由语篇交际目的决定的,即为对外宣传"一带一路"倡议营造出客观中立、平等协商、和谐包容的对话空间,赢得读者尊重和信任,影响读者阅读立场,建立作者与读者的评价同盟,引导读者接受作者观点;"五通"发展旨在造福"一带一路"沿线的国家和民众,本着共建共享、互惠互利的精神,中国和沿线国家不遗余力推动"五通"发展,合作成果显著,未来发展潜力巨大。

第六,中欧"一带一路"对外新闻更注重人品说服的修辞策略,较大篇幅运用判断资源和主导型韵律模式报道中国和欧洲各国领导人的外交言论,体现他们高瞻远瞩的政治觉悟和一心为民的治国理念;中亚"一带一路"对外新闻更注重逻辑说服的修辞策略,较大篇幅运用鉴赏资源和增强型韵律模式报道中国和亚洲各国的合作领域、方式和层次,体现区域合作的巨大潜力和重大意义;中非"一带一路"对外新闻更注重情感说服的修辞策略,较大篇幅运用情感资源和渗透型韵律模式报道非洲各国加入"一带一路"建设的强烈愿望,以及对该倡议的赞赏和信任,强调该倡议在非洲大陆的历史文化背景,尤其是对非洲普通民众的意义,体现"一带一路"在非洲逐渐深入人心,建立了坚实的民意基础;中拉"一带一路"对外新闻更注重逻辑说服的修辞策略,较大篇幅运用鉴赏资源和增强型韵律模式报道中国与拉美各国合作项目的潜力和意义,体现"一带一路"建设和拉美地区的发展需求高度契合。

　　本研究的意义在于，第一，扩展"一带一路"对外新闻语篇的研究维度，揭示了各种介入和态度话语资源在该类新闻语篇中的分布规律、话语韵律的人际意义、交际目的和修辞功能。第二，加深欧洲、亚洲、非洲和拉美地区读者对"一带一路"倡议的理解，尤其是发展"五通"旨在造福"一带一路"沿线的国家和民众，唤起情感共鸣，促进该倡议深入民心，推动"五通"目标顺利实现。第三，帮助新闻从业人员撰写"一带一路"对外新闻，增强此类新闻对沿线不同地区读者的区分度和针对性，提高该倡议的对外宣传效果。

目　录

功能语言学在人际意义研究中丰富发展起来的"词汇—语法框架",与语篇的对话性有着内在的联系。

"一带一路"倡议虽然由中国提出,但"一带一路"事业属于全人类,是全球瞩目的话题,因此,关于"一带一路"倡议的新闻报道备受世人关注。本研究按照习总书记在党的十九大报告中关于中国对外话语权的讲话精神,主要以评价理论和古典修辞理论为理论框架,以"一带一路"对外英文新闻为研究语料,揭示"一带一路"对外新闻语篇结构中各部分介入和态度话语资源的分布规律,阐明韵律话语策略在"一带一路"对外新闻语料中的交际功能和人际意义,揭示"一带一路"对外新闻语篇的韵律话语模式和修辞说服策略。

我们用以下一篇"一带一路"对外新闻报道为例子,通过分析来阐明本研究所关心的问题和研究方法。该语篇来自中国国家英文日报 *China Daily*(2018 年 7 月 11 日)。

Belt and Road Initiative culmination of China's reform and opening-up

Thanks to the vision and role of Deng Xiaoping, China took the historically bold initiative of economic reform and opening-up in 1978. This year China is celebrating the 40th anniversary of the reform and opening-up. Philosopher Confucius, who has been a huge influence on Chinese society, once said, "At 40, I had no doubts". It is said that

提出,为中国的制度性国际话语权建设带来了希望(王义桅,2016);"一带一路"倡议的全面推进为我国对外传播事业提供了难得的历史机遇(史安斌、盛阳,2017);通过"一带一路"倡议的推进,中国与沿途国家间将进一步增强政治互信、文化融合和经济依存,增进沿途国家对中国文化、中国话语体系和价值观的认同,助力中国国际话语权和话语体系的提升和完善(刘再起、王蔓莉,2016);传播平台很重要,对外传播能力的大小在话语权构建中扮演着至关重要的角色(王秋彬、崔庭赫,2015)。可见,对外新闻作为对外传播的重要平台,既能为"一带一路"建设创造有利的国际舆论环境,也能推动我国国际传播能力建设,从而促进国际话语权的构建。

随着"一带一路"建设的持续推进,新闻媒体在对外宣传政策和报道建设成果方面至关重要。在新闻报道中,新闻作者不是简单地陈述新闻事件,而是广泛引用他人话语,通过外在声音向读者阐述新闻事件的真实性和重要性,以及实现新闻语篇的人际功能。而新闻报道中各种声音并存,形成相互作用关系,此起彼伏,遥相呼应,具有广泛的对话性。尚智慧(2011)指出,对话性是新闻语篇的本质属性,体现了新闻语篇的客观性,与此同时,对话性还帮助构建了新闻语篇意欲传达的意识形态。Bakhtin(1984)指出,对话性是指语篇中存在两个以上相互作用的声音,它们形成同意或反对、肯定和补充、问与答等关系。Martin 和 White 受 Bakhtin 对话性和Kristeva 互文性的影响,创立了评价理论。评价理论是系统社会的认可和支持;同时,"一带一路"建设带动了沿线国家的经济合作和文化交流,提升了中国的区域影响力,也为中国增强对外话语权提供了难得的机遇和有利条件。而对外新闻是推动"一带一路"建设的国际传播途径,是对外话语体系的重要成分,也是增强对外话语权的必要手段,其重要性毋庸置疑。

"一带一路"是"丝绸之路经济带"和"21世纪海上丝绸之路"的简称,是中国国家主席习近平在2013年9月和10月出访中亚和东南亚国家期间提出来的。古代丝绸之路就是中国和沿线国家政治、经济、贸易、文化交流的共同舞台。"一带一路"倡议传承古代丝绸之路的开放、包容、合作精神,并结合世界多极化、经济全球化,赋予其新的时代内涵,充分依靠中国与有关国家既有的双多边机制,借助既有的、行之有效的区域合作平台,高举和平发展的旗帜,积极发展与沿线国家的经济合作伙伴关系,共同打造政治互信、经济融合、文化包容的利益共同体、命运共同体和责任共同体。

对外新闻是向世界宣传"一带一路"倡议的重要窗口,是中国主动设置议题、传播议题、参与国际社会话语互动的重要途径,也是我国建构对外话语体系和国际话语权的重要媒介。目前,我国国际话语权仍处于"结构性"弱势地位,我国国家形象更多是"他塑"而非"自塑",因此更需要对外传播媒体改变国际舆论场上我国的弱势地位,提升我国的影响力和传播力,塑造好国家形象(董媛媛、田晨,2017)。而"一带一路"倡议的

第一章 绪 论

一、研究背景

　　2017年10月18日,习近平总书记在党的十九大上做了题为《决胜全面建成小康社会 夺取新时代中国特色社会主义伟大胜利》的报告。在关于中国对外话语权的讲话中,习总书记指出,要提高中国对外话语权,就要"推进国际传播能力建设,讲好中国故事,展现真实、立体、全面的中国,提高国家文化软实力"。在报告中,习总书记五次提到了"一带一路"相关内容,指出"一带一路"倡议对我国以及世界的政治、经济、文化、外交等方面都有重大意义。

　　2016年12月,中央全面深化改革领导小组第三十次会议审议通过的《关于加强"一带一路"软力量建设的指导意见》提出,"加强理论研究和话语体系建设,推进舆论宣传和舆论引导工作,加强国际传播能力建设,为'一带一路'建设提供有力理论支撑、舆论支持、文化条件"。由此可见,实施"一带一路"倡议需要加强对外话语体系建设,从而为该倡议赢得国际

China experienced a lot more in the last 40 years than at any other time. The Belt and Road Initiative, new vision of President Xi Jinping for China and the rest of the world, has been recognized as a new historical culmination of reform and opening-up to make China Dream a success and to contribute to success for rest of the world.

Professor Kerry Brown of King's College London said, "Understanding China's past reforms and with it the basis for China's success is also important for China's future reforms—understanding the path traveled, the circumstances under which historical decisions were made and what their effects were on the course of China's economy will inform decision-makers on where to go next." Actually, this analysis and reflection on the last reform and opening-up is not only significant for the China but also for rest of the world. From past four decades to until now, China's economic influence in the international arena has dramatically increased. Many countries want to learn and follow Chinese path of development. For them, Chinese model of development could show the way to modernize nations and resolve structural problems and play a prominent role in the global spheres managing domestic challenges. At the 19th Party congress President Xi said on

China's success, "It means that the path, theory, the system, and the culture of socialism with Chinese characteristics have kept developing, blazing a new trail for other developing countries to achieve modernization. It offers a new option for other countries and nations who want to speed up their development while preserving their independence; and it offers Chinese wisdom and a Chinese approach to solving the problems facing mankind."

Some scholars say that China's developmental path is a miracle. But for me, that is not true. Present situation is a result of systematic and farsighted gradual reform process. Chinese leadership from central to local level realizing ground reality of local, central and global spheres, prepared themselves to move forward. This is why they succeeded in taking on challenges and wrote a successful story. "Crossing the river by feeling the stones" was a popular dictum for Chinese leadership at the mid-1980s to learn and act through experiences. "Decisions of CPC Central Committee on Some Issues Concerning the Establishment of a Socialist Market Economic Structure" in 1993 further opened a new chapter to take grand initiative to hype reform process and penned more success stories.

At the Boao Forum for Asia a few months ago,

President Xi highlighting the importance of reform process said that today, the Chinese people can say with great pride that reform and opening-up, China's "second revolution", has not only profoundly changed the country but also greatly influenced the world. Knowing the Xi Jinping thought, many China watchers now say that BRI is the new climax on the systematic journey of reform and opening-up. By launching BRI in 2013, it aims to contribute for inclusive economic governance, development, peace, harmony and people-to-people contacts in the global arena. Through this spirit, Chinese leaders have been taking important steps with amending constitution this year and President Xi and his team are completely prepared to enhance and implement further spirit of reform and opening-up based on domestic and global circumstances.

Definitely, it is no easy task to continue reform and opening-up. There are multiple challenges in the world and will continue to exist. Particularly, with the ascendancy of Donald Trump in the US leadership, one by one he is taking decisions against the spirit of globalization, free trade, global cooperation, climate change and global responsibility. He has taken "protectionism" as a basic principle to make his country "Great Again". This new deviation of American leadership creates historical problems to sustain global peace, development and cooperation on multiple fronts. "A new model of major-power relations" was the term used by Chinese side in 2013 to address the US-China relationship. But US is still not ready to accept this term. American authorities do not easily accept any countries like China to take prominent economic and political role in the global sphere. So they use the term "China Threat" as an important aspect of foreign and security policy. This is why American people elected hardliner conservative candidate Donald Trump.

Since the launch of BRI, it has attracted worldwide attention and sent positive message of cooperation to build the harmonious world based on mutual trust and win-win cooperation. President Xi described it as the "project of the century". It is estimated that it could affect over 4. 4 billion people in more than 70 countries and cover a GDP of over $ 23 trillion once it is completed. China has already given signals to invest more than $ 1. 25 trillion in multiple projects. Within a short span of time, BRI has succeeded in impressing various governments, enterprises, business communities and common people too. BRI has also taken important instruments to achieve the two "century goals" of

China and to advance hands of cooperation and partnership with the world community.

Last four decades in Chinese history show that only the reform and opening-up was the vital initiative to achieve present prosperity, peace and harmony in the Chinese nation. Due to the strong leadership at the top to implement agendas of reform and opening-up, even with fighting many internal and external challenges, China has pragmatically gained this present status in the global stages. Now new challenges in the global economic, political and security spheres are emerging. There is no easy way ahead to cope alone with domestic and global spheres for all states of global community. So China has proposed BRI and concept of the "community of common destiny for mankind" to take massive international responsibility based on mutual trust and win-win cooperation to resolve the common challenges and create the better harmonious world. The year 2018 will be the great historical time for the Chinese leadership to take bold commitment on further enhancement of spirit of reform and opening-up based on the requirement of domestic and global circumstances.

该报道围绕"一带一路"的三方面进行阐述：(1)"一带一

路"倡议是中国 40 年改革开放政策的延续和发展,是继往开来、开拓创新的国家政策;(2)"一带一路"倡议为全世界提供了中国智慧和中国方案,致力于构建人类命运共同体;(3)"一带一路"倡议面临的国际挑战和发展机遇。

该语篇作者运用介入资源,为语篇中不同声音构建话语空间,通过协调不同观点,与读者建立同盟关系,影响读者的阅读立场。该新闻开篇阶段,即标题和头两句,作者只呈现一种声音,话语空间是封闭的,表明其内容是毋庸置疑,不容协商的:"一带一路"倡议是中国改革开放发展的新阶段;邓小平的远见卓识造就了中国大胆的经济改革;40 年改革开放硕果累累。随后两小句中,作者通过引述"Philosopher Confucius … once said …"和"It is said …"打开话语空间,为不同声音搭建对话平台,表明新闻语篇开放包容的话语立场和客观公正的报道视角,首先转述孔子话语"四十不惑",然后通过匿名引述,表明中国经过 40 年改革开放积累了经验,坚定了信念,佐证了"四十不惑"。作者在引述孔子话语时,通过定语从句指明孔子对中国社会的巨大影响,旨在增强引述对象的权威性,提高引述内容的可信度,力求影响读者的阅读立场,说服读者认可引述内容,接受语篇话语立场,最终潜移默化地建立作者和读者的同盟关系。第一段的最后一句中,作者通过"… has been recognized …"压缩了对话空间,表明"一带一路"倡议是习近平为中国和世界绘制的发展蓝图,是中国改革开放进程的新阶段,是实现中国梦和世界繁荣的重要途径。综观第一

段,作者通过介入资源,有策略地调控语篇话语空间,首先呈现一个封闭话语空间,只有作者自己的声音,把其他声音拒之门外,然后打开话语空间,欢迎多种声音进入其中,最后压缩话语空间,再次突显作者自己的声音。此种话语策略反映了语篇的人际意义:开篇明确表达作者立场,奠定评价基调;然后引述他人话语,营造客观中立的话语氛围,引导读者接受语篇的评价姿态;最后强调作者立场,巩固与读者的同盟关系。语篇第二段的话语策略有所不同,话语空间更加开放。作者首先通过"said"引述知名学者,表明这只是该学者的一家之言,从而扩展话语空间,引入多种声音;然后通过"actually"和"not only … but also"阐述引述内容的深刻含义,表明作者承认读者对引述内容(即中国的改革开放只利于中国)有不同理解,并欢迎持不同见解的读者进入对话空间,一起磋商立场,从而在某种程度上赢得了他们的尊重,增强了语篇内容的说服力,为随后提出的自己见解(即中国的改革开放不仅利于中国,而且造福全世界)赢得更多支持。如此一来,话语空间从扩展变为压缩,从引入多种声音,到突显自己声音,作者既展现了新闻语篇开放包容的立场,也通过磋商扩大并巩固了自己和读者的同盟关系。随后,作者通过"could"和"said"再次扩展对话空间,表明中国发展模式可能有助于其他国家实现现代化,解决经济结构问题,应对国内和国际挑战,但这只是一种可能性,暗指存在其他不同的声音和立场。最后,通过直接引述习主席的话语,不仅再现新闻语篇客观公正的报道立

场,增强报道内容的可信度,而且强化作者的立场(即中国发展模式是史无前例的,为其他发展中国家树立了榜样,为全人类共同问题提供了中国智慧和中国方案)。

综观第二段,话语空间从扩展到压缩再到扩展,此种策略反映出作者通过介入资源不断与读者对话,磋商立场,建立同盟,以便说服读者接受作者观点。

语篇第三段的话语空间进一步压缩直至关闭。作者首先通过"say"展开话语空间,随即通过"But"和"not"连续压缩话语空间,之后就关闭对话空间,只呈现作者自己的声音。通过引述某些学者的话语,作者旨在澄清误解,表明中国的发展道路不是奇迹,而是缜密部署、水到渠成的过程,体现了中国政府领导人的远见卓识和稳健作风。作者的语篇在充分考虑不同声音后,阐明自己立场,既包容开放,又独立思考,逻辑严密,有理有据,从而赢得读者的认同,建立广泛而坚定的同盟关系。

语篇第四段延续了第三段的话语策略,先使用"highlighting"和"… can say…"扩展话语空间,然后通过"not only… but also"压缩话语空间,直到最后关闭话语空间。此种先扩展后压缩直至关闭对话空间的话语策略,其目的是博得读者认同,影响读者阅读立场,与读者建立同盟。

语篇第五段继续压缩话语空间,"Definitely"表明作者明确支持随后小句的内容(即继续改革开放并不容易),通过突显某一观点而压缩对话空间;"no easy task"表明作者已经预

料到部分读者以为继续改革开放是容易的,作者明确表示这样的观点是错误的,如此一来,作者向读者展现了自己周到的考虑、缜密的思维和明确的立场,通过否定某一观点而压缩对话空间;"Particularly"把语篇内容聚焦在美国总统特朗普的"保护主义"政策以及其对全球和平、发展与合作造成的问题,通过突显中美之间的差异而排除其他分歧,从而压缩对话空间;"But,still,not,do not"连续否定部分读者的立场,以压缩对话空间。综观第五段,作者反复运用突显某一观点和否定某一观点的介入策略,以持续压缩对话空间。

语篇第六段,作者基本关闭了对话空间,只用一种声音展现"一带一路"所取得的成就,只有在展望"一带一路"未来发展时,作者用"It is estimated…"和"could"短暂打开了对话空间,随后又立即关闭了对话空间。

语篇最后一段,作者依然是压缩对话空间,"only"突显了改革开放的重要性,指出改革开放是取得繁荣、和平与和谐的唯一途径,通过突显改革开放,而淡化其他立场,以压缩对话空间;同样,通过"no easy way",作者引入一种立场,即独自应对国内外问题是容易的,然后果断否定这一立场,压缩对话空间,从而进一步突显作者立场。

与此同时,该语篇作者也运用丰富的态度资源,来赞赏"一带一路"倡议,肯定中国国家领导人的远见卓识和务实才干。

作者两次用"vision"塑造邓小平和习近平两代领导人一

脉相承的睿智创新,邓小平带领中国于 1978 年开始改革开放,40 年来取得举世瞩目的成功,中国的经济、文化、政治和社会其他方面都实现了历史性的飞跃。40 年后的今天,习近平代表中国向全世界推进"一带一路"倡议,旨在 40 年中国改革开放的经验基础上,把改革开放推向高潮,促进实现"中国梦"和世界共同繁荣。在传达态度时,作者不仅用词汇资源直接表达对新闻人物和事件的评价立场(vision, bold, a huge influence),而且通过小句间接激发引导读者的阅读立场(This year China is celebrating the 40th anniversary of the reform and opening-up)。作者通过追溯历史开启语篇,用"vision"和"bold"塑造邓小平作为中国改革开放奠基人和总工程师的形象,"vision"修饰对象是邓小平,"bold"虽然是改革开放政策的定语,但在此小句中能引发读者对该政策提出者的积极评价。随后小句"This year China is celebrating the 40th anniversary of the reform and opening-up"中"celebrating"表明改革开放政策在过去 40 年取得了成功,从而促使读者对于中国政府 40 年来的工作进行正面评价。随后,作者引用孔子的话"四十不惑",并用"a huge influence"来表明孔子在中国社会的地位,结合小句"China experienced a lot more in the last 40 years than at any other time"阐明中国在 40 年改革开放中积累了丰富经验,从而把中国描绘成历史悠久、锐意进取的开放国度;通过援引孔子的"四十不惑",表明中国经过 40 年的实践,对改革开放坚信不疑,将要一张蓝图绘到底,继续坚持改革开放。回顾过去之后,作者聚焦当代,用"new vision"修饰习近平主席,表明习主席对邓小平的改革开放政策既是一脉相承,又是深化创新,又用"for China and the rest of the world"展现习近平的深谋远虑、宽广视野,作者用小句"The Belt and Road Initiative … has been recognized as a new historical culmination of reform and opening-up"把"一带一路"倡议展现为被广泛认可的、具有历史根基和与时俱进的政策,随后通过"make China Dream a success"和"contribute to success for rest of the world"描绘了"一带一路"倡议立足中国梦、放眼全世界的宏伟蓝图。可见,作者在该新闻语篇首段中,通过词汇语法手段,赞赏邓小平和习近平两代领导人的远见卓识,肯定中国改革开放 40 年的成功经验,阐明"一带一路"倡议是改革开放政策的延续和推进,虽然由中国提出,但是旨在实现全人类的共同发展。

该新闻语篇第二段着重描述中国发展模式,即中国特色社会主义,对全世界发展中国家的积极影响。作者首先引用伦敦国王学院 Kerry Brown 教授的话,表明中国改革的成功经验影响中国未来的发展方向;随后指出中国在国际上的经济影响力快速增强,这促使很多发展中国家想要效仿中国的发展模式,最后援引习近平在十九大报告中的话,强调中国特色社会主义是朝气蓬勃、不断创新的社会制度,有助于发展中国家实现独立自主的现代化目标,为全人类共同面临的问题贡献中国智慧和中国方案。作者通过"significant, dramatically increased, prominent, developing, blazing a new trail, wisdom"等词汇来传达其对中国发展模式的态度：中国成功的改革不仅影响中国的未来发展，而且是所有发展中国家的榜样，有助于应对全人类的共同挑战，由此，中国的"负责任大国"形象跃然纸上。

在第三段中，新闻作者毫不掩饰自己的态度，通过"But for me"向读者阐明自己的见解：中国的发展道路并非奇迹，而是极具远见、有条不紊、水到渠成的改革过程。中国领导层从中央到地方，深知当地现实，了解全国状况，把握全球趋势，因此应对挑战时，思路清晰，心中有数。作者把中国的改革成就归功于中国领导层的脚踏实地和远见卓识。作者不惜赞美之词，用"systematic, farsighted"修饰改革过程，暗示中国领导人不仅有愿景目标，而且有规划统筹；用"succeeded, successful, grand, success"突显中国领导层敢于担当，积极进取，成绩斐然。

第四段聚焦习近平主席在博鳌论坛的讲话，再次强调改革开放的重要性：不仅给中国带来翻天覆地的变化，而且对世界造成深远影响。作者援引中国问题研究者的话语指出，"一带一路"倡议把改革开放进程推向新高潮，旨在为全球经济发展、人类和平共存做出贡献，为此，以习近平为核心的中国政府领导层准备继续深化改革，扩大开放，着眼国内，放眼国际。作者用"with great pride"表现中国人民对改革开放的骄傲之情，用"profoundly"和"greatly"展现改革开放对中国和世界

产生的积极影响,用"systematic"和"climax"体现"一带一路"倡议是改革开放政策的继承和发展,用"contribute, inclusive, peace, harmony, global"点明"一带一路"倡议是旨在促进全球经济发展,实现全人类和谐繁荣,具有包容性的开放政策,用"taking important steps, completely prepared"展现习近平带领的中国政府高效工作,准备充分,坚定不移地继续执行改革开放政策。

第五段集中描述美国总统唐纳德·特朗普的"保护主义"政策,以及其对维护全球和平、发展、合作构成的问题和挑战。与中国的"一带一路"倡议形成鲜明对比的是,美国领导层做出的一系列决定,都违背了全球化、自由贸易、各国合作等精神,旨在通过自我保护实现重新崛起,美国政府不愿意看到中国在世界经济和政治舞台上的影响力与日俱增,试图通过杜撰"中国威胁论"来遏制中国的发展。新闻作者用"no easy task, multiple challenges"来突显深化改革开放所面临的种种困难,用"against the spirit, deviation, problems, hardliner"来表现美国政府的"利己主义",这与中国"一带一路"倡议所倡导的"开放包容,利益共享"形成鲜明反差,最后用两个小句"American authorities do not easily accept any countries like China to take prominent economic and political role in the global sphere. So they use the term 'China Threat' as an important aspect of foreign and security policy"显示美国当局心胸狭窄,傲慢自大。

　　为了与美国的"单边主义"进行对比,作者在第六段中重点阐述"一带一路"倡议的多元化、包容性和普适性。作者用"worldwide, positive, harmonious, mutual, win-win"来阐明"一带一路"倡议旨在通过各国合作,建立互信,实现双赢,构建和谐世界,用一系列数字来呈现"一带一路"倡议的发展规模和影响力,用"short, succeeded, impressing, various"来说明"一带一路"倡议在各国政府、企业和百姓中已经得到广泛认可,最后,通过小句再次重申该倡议不仅力求实现中国的"两个一百年"奋斗目标,而且推动全世界的合作发展。

　　在该新闻语篇的最后一段中,作者指出中国目前的繁荣、和平与和谐都归功于改革开放政策,以及中国政府领导层的有效执行力。为了应对全球经济、政治和安全领域的新挑战,中国提出"一带一路"倡议和"人类命运共同体"概念,旨在建立互信双赢的合作关系,共同承担国际责任,解决共同的挑战,创造和谐的世界。作者用"vital, achieve, prosperity, peace, harmony"指明改革开放的重要性,用"strong, fighting, pragmatically, gain"表现中国领导层的治国理政能力出众,实施政策务实有效,用"new challenges, massive responsibility"呈现世界面临的挑战,和中国承担的责任,最后用"bold commitment, further enhancement"展现中国政府勇于面对挑战,继续改革开放,为全球发展做出贡献,从而塑造出中国"负责任大国"的国际形象。

二、研究目的和意义

目的:本书以评价理论和古典修辞理论为理论框架,结合新闻语篇结构模型,分析中国一带一路网、*China Daily* 和 Xinhua News Agency 上的对外英文新闻语料,旨在探讨"一带一路"对外新闻语篇如何运用介入策略构建出独特的韵律话语模式,为对外宣传"一带一路"倡议营造出平等协商、和谐包容的对话空间,推进实现"五通"目标,以及态度策略如何通过态度韵律实现修辞功能,即通过渗透型、主导型和增强型韵律模式,实现情感说服、人品说服和逻辑说服。

理论意义:由语言学家 Martin 建立的评价理论是以系统功能语言学为基础,是研究语篇中词汇语义层面上人际意义的一个重要理论。目前,鲜有学者将该理论应用于"一带一路"对外新闻的语篇研究。本研究主要选取中国新闻媒体上的对外英文新闻语料,分析各类介入和态度资源在此类语篇中的分布规律,阐释话语韵律策略在"一带一路"对外新闻语篇中的交际功能和人际意义。这不仅能扩展评价理论介入系统和态度系统的应用范围,也能丰富对外新闻话语分析的理论体系。

实践意义:本书通过研究"一带一路"对外新闻中开篇、详述、解释、背景和评论五部分的介入和态度资源的分布特点,发现新闻作者在各部分应用不同的介入和态度策略是为了达

到不同的交际目的和修辞功能,对读者产生不同的影响。通过相关文献的阅读和初步分析,我们预测"一带一路"对外新闻的介入策略随着语篇各阶段交际目的的变化将表现出韵律话语模式,为对外宣传"一带一路"倡议构建出开放包容的对话空间,以及态度策略在语篇各阶段通过不同的韵律话语模式,分别实现情感说服、人品说服和逻辑说服的修辞功能,从而推动该倡议在沿线各国深入人心,促进"五通"目标的顺利实现。本研究有助于读者更深入解读"一带一路"对外新闻语篇的话语策略,有助于新闻从业人员撰写"一带一路"对外新闻,提高对外宣传效果。

三、研究语料、研究方法和研究思路

(一)研究语料

本研究从中国一带一路网、*China Daily* 和 Xinhua News Agency 上选取 2015 年 5 月至 2019 年 5 月期间 400 篇对外英文新闻作为研究语料,体裁涵盖会议报道、政策通告、事件要闻、宣传成果和历史文化,并从"五通"目标方面各选一篇素材,从中欧、中亚、中非和中拉发展角度各选一篇语料进行具体语篇分析,探究介入资源和态度资源在此类新闻语篇中的分布规律,以及介入和态度策略的韵律话语模式、修辞功能和人际意义。

(二)研究方法

本研究采取定量分析和定性分析相结合的研究方法。首先使用定量分析法对新闻语篇中的介入和态度资源进行分类、统计，揭示各种资源在语篇不同部分中的分布规律，然后通过具体实例分析数据，再通过定性分析解释这些分布规律所体现的话语韵律模式、修辞功能和人际意义。

(三)研究思路

本研究遵循"文献综述—理论框架与研究语料—定量分析—定性分析"的思路来构建全书，如图 1-1 所示。

四、本书结构

第一章为绪论，简要介绍本书的研究背景、研究目的和意义，以及研究语料和研究方法。

第二章为文献综述，梳理和评述了评价理论的介入系统和态度系统、新闻结构、修辞功能和"一带一路"新闻语篇研究的现状，并在此基础上提出了本书的研究方向。

第三章为理论框架，介绍了本书的理论基础，即评价理论的介入系统和态度系统、古典修辞理论和新闻结构模型。

第四章为"一带一路"对外新闻介入策略定量分析，研究此类新闻语篇结构各部分介入资源的分布规律，揭示了介入策略在语篇中的韵律话语模式。

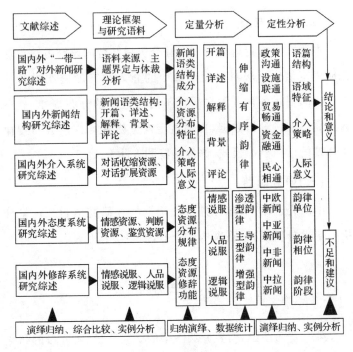

图 1-1　研究思路

第五章为"一带一路"对外新闻介入策略定性分析,从"五通"发展的角度分别选取一篇对外新闻语篇进行具体分析,探究其介入资源的分布规律以及介入策略所蕴含的人际意义和交际目的。

第六章为"一带一路"对外新闻态度策略定量分析,对语篇的态度资源进行统计和分析,探究态度韵律在语篇结构中的发展模式,揭示其修辞说服策略。

第七章为"一带一路"对外新闻态度策略定性分析,选取针对欧洲、非洲、亚洲和拉美地区的"一带一路"对外新闻实例进行分析,进一步论证态度资源是如何实现其修辞功能。

第八章为本书的结论部分,总结了本研究结果,并点明了研究中的不足以及对今后研究的一些建议。

第二章　文献综述

在经济全球化和世界多极化的国际背景下,"一带一路"倡议不仅促进了沿线国家的发展,也在国际社会上发挥了日益显著的作用。随着"一带一路"倡议的实施,媒体在推动政策传达和执行过程中扮演着重要角色,因此越来越多的学者对相关媒体报道进行了不同方面和不同程度的研究。本章将对前人关于评价理论介入系统和态度系统、修辞功能、新闻结构以及"一带一路"新闻语篇的研究进行分析与总结,从而为本书奠定研究基础。

一、评价理论的研究

评价理论是对系统功能语言学的新发展,属于阐释性理论。任教于澳大利亚悉尼大学语言学系的语言学家 James R. Martin 在 20 世纪 90 年代发展了系统功能语言学,创立了评价系统的理论框架。Martin 和 Rose(2002)指出,作为语义系统的评价理论,旨在探讨、描绘、揭示交际中作者/说话者如何通过语言资源来确定立场、评价态度、建构角色和磋商关系,从而与观点相似的读者/听者结成同盟,努力说服持不同立场或犹豫不决的交际者,疏远或排斥持相反观点的对话参与者,最终实现话语交际目的。Martin 和 White(2005)将评价理论分为三个系统:介入系统、态度系统和级差系统。本书主要从介入系统和态度系统视角分析"一带一路"对外新闻语篇,本小节先评述介入系统的相关文献,然后综述态度系统的相关研究成果。

关于介入系统,国外和国内学者都对其开展了理论探讨,并运用介入系统对各类语篇进行话语分析。

在国外,介入系统可追溯到 Bakhtin(1984)对语言对话性的阐述和 Kristeva(1986)有关语篇互文性的解读。从社会言语交际互动的观点出发,Bakhtin(1984)提出了对话理论。Bakhtin 把对话的概念从狭义的面对面交际扩展为广义的任何言语交际形式,包括任何通过言语行为来实现的人们意识形态观念的对话。这样,在一个话语中人们对同一对象的相同或不同的观念、评价等都可以被视为是一种对话。Bakhtin(1984)指出,话语具有内在的对话性,任何一个具体的话语都是特定领域中的言语交际链条上的一环,言语交际是多方面积极的"思想交流"过程,它们彼此熟悉,相互反应。后来,语言学家 Kristeva(1986)发展了 Bakhtin 的对话理论,她认为,所有语篇都是由引语整合而成的,每个语篇都是吸收和转换其他语篇的结果,因此任何语篇本质上都具有互文性。Martin(1992)认为,介入系统中许多作为模糊限制语的资源根本就不是用来表示怀疑或含糊,而是承认某个命题的可争议性,表明愿意和持异议者进行协商或对其表示尊重,这些资源具有重要的人际功能。Voloshinov(1995)认为,对话不仅仅指人与人之间直接的、面对面的、发声的口头交际,也可以指任何一种形式的言语交际,比如一本书或一个出版物的言语行为,都是言语交际的一部分,这种言语行为好像在进行大规模的意识形态的对话:它回应、确认、预料可能的反应和异议,并寻求支持。介入系统重视读者所发挥的作用,将语篇看作是和实际的或潜在的读者协商意义的方式。White(1998)继承了 Martin 的观点,将因果和让步连词归入介入系统,在承认其逻辑衔接功能的前提下,进一步突出了其人际功能。语言学传统从形式逻辑的角度解释否定,认为肯定和否定是平等对立的价值,而 White(1998)借鉴了 Pagano(1994)和 Fairclough(1992)等人的观点,从人际的角度解释归一度的语义:因为否定包含肯定的可能,而肯定只是指自己,所以否定比肯定负载更多的人际价值。Bakhtin(1981)在 *The Dialogic Imagination* 一书中讨论了对话性和多语性,他认为,语言是一个由说话者的社会言语相互作用而实现的不断形成过程,语言在其实际的实现过程中,不可分割地与意识形态或生活内容联系在一起。Bakhtin(1981)认为,听话人不仅仅是在消极被动地接受和理解互动中的言语,同时也在积极地应对,听话人有可能同意或不同意所听到的言语,也有可能补充它、应用它等。说话者和听话者是话语的共同创造者。

当听者补充或应用所听到的言语时，听者则变为言者。Thompson 和 Hunston(2000)认为，评价有三个功能，其中一个就是评价可以构建和保持说话者/作者与听话者/读者之间的关系。这一点也可以从 White 的"介入系统"所采取的视角可以看出。White(2003)指出，以前关于情态和传信性的研究认为，这些表达方式的唯一功能在于揭示说话者/作者的心理状态或者知识状况，表明说话者/作者对陈述命题真值的不确定和不负责任。而他则要验证这些表达的对话功能性，并从这种对话的视角分析这些语言表达在构建说话者和听话者之间关系中的作用。Martin(2005)把语言对话性和语篇互文性引入介入系统，认为交际者运用语言介入资源协商和调整语篇内外各种声音之间的对话潜势。在 Martin 和 White(2005)的评价理论框架下，介入系统分为单声和多声。单声不提及对话的替代声音，而多声则允许不同的声音存在。考虑到话语的主观性和客观性，单声表达了说话者/作者的主观性，而多声在某种程度上引发讨论，体现客观性。

在国内，张德禄(1998)是第一位提到评价理论的学者。直到王振华(2001)在他的论文中介绍了评价理论，评价理论才开始引起很多研究者的关注。在介入系统研究方面，王振华做出了显著贡献。王振华(2003)以心理学、社会学和语义学理论为基础重新建构了介入系统的构架。他把介入系统分成三个"声音"。第一声是指言语者在特定语境中投射言语者自身的思想或观点。第二声指言语者在特定环境中假借第二人称或第三人称的思想或观点。第三声指言语者在特定语言环境中假借所在社团共享的思想或观点。刘世铸和韩金龙（2004）认为，评价可以分为文本内和文本外评价，Martin 的评价体系只是在话语中的评价。李战子（2004）通过分析《论不说汉语》一书中对"中国人特质"的评价，发现了评价的矛盾和多声现象，并指出这是作者对中国人特质的一种矛盾立场。刘世铸（2007）提出，主体间性是构建话语的核心部分。话语中的交际互动为增进说话者和听话者的理解奠定了基础，因此，主体间性研究非常有意义。马伟林（2007）认为，Martin 的介入系统源于 Bakhtin 的复调理论，该系统不仅停留在人际功能中的认知情态、言据性和模糊语上，涵盖表示可能性和常规性的情态，而且研究作者如何协调自己的声音和其他人的声音、如何调节自己的立场和读者的立场。作者在表明自己观点的同时也请求其他人同意他的观点，这种对话性质使得读者分享作者的价值观和信仰。李基安（2008）把情态视作重要的介入资源，探讨了情态的对话本质以及情态的级差与对话空间的关系。王振华和路洋（2010）对介入系统的发展进行了回顾，认为介入的目的是描述和解释话语中的资源，实现主体间的交流——这是对介入系统相对综合的评价。江晓红（2011）介绍了介入系统及其语言手段，讨论了介入体现出来的语篇内部不同立场之间的互动或协商。

除了理论探讨以外，国内学者也运用介入系统对不同类型语篇进行话语分析。唐丽萍（2005）从对话的视角对学术书评微妙复杂的评价策略做介入分析。通过对 10 篇语言学书评评价阶段的自言资源进行统计,发现自言资源呈现不同的运用频率,而且在赞扬和批评之间呈现出不同的介入倾向:样本语篇中最充分利用的自言资源为可能性、意料之中和意料之外,其次为否定和求证,而很少利用传闻和宣称;宣言和求证更多用来表达赞扬策略,弃言更多用来表达批评策略,可能性和传闻未呈现出上述明显倾向。潘小珏(2008)用评价理论的介入系统作为理论框架分析法庭辩论话语,比较各种介入资源的使用及其在说服过程中的作用,探讨辩论双方怎样通过引用观点的来源展示自己的看法,归纳法庭辩论中为实现对法官的说服可采取的策略。研究发现,介入资源在法庭辩论中得到广泛运用,辩论双方可通过构建事实和表明立场来说明己方观点,反驳对方观点,进而说服法官做出对己方有利的判决。袁传有(2008)运用评价理论所建构的警察讯问介入系统,分析三起刑事案件的讯问笔录,并阐释警察在讯问不同类型的犯罪嫌疑人时所采用的介入模式和所体现的人际意义,即立场、态度和观点。研究发现,警察在讯问故意杀人的犯罪嫌疑人时,常用对话紧缩的介入模式,限制犯罪嫌疑人的话语空间;而面对由家庭暴力的受虐者演变而来的犯罪嫌疑人时,介入的方式则比较复杂。当犯罪嫌疑人被主观地认定有犯罪的故意时,警察多用对话紧缩策略来表达怀疑、训斥的态度。而当犯罪嫌疑人正处于家庭暴力的威胁下,被迫采取以暴制暴行为时,警察更多使用对话延展的介入模式,以表达同情的态度,并鼓励犯罪嫌疑人为自己的行为辩护。李君和张德禄(2010)以评价理论的介入系统为分析框架,通过对中央电视台《对话》节目访谈语篇的分析,探索电视新闻访谈的显著介入特征。研究结果表明:访谈的叙述、提问和回答部分的介入特征既有相似性又有差异性,受电视新闻访谈语类和语域特点的影响,电视新闻访谈各部分介入特征的交错互动形成了显著的韵律性模式。介入资源的合理运用可以为整个访谈营造一个互动、协商的空间,帮助访谈者进行有效的提问,树立嘉宾的权威。林美珍(2011)以评价理论中的介入系统为理论框架,分析了农业语篇中介入资源的分布特征,说明介入资源的使用与语类有着密切的关系。研究结果表明:(1)紧缩资源和扩展资源在语料库中呈现不均衡分布。其中扩展资源的使用比率明显高于紧缩资源的比率。基本上符合学术论文摘要追求客观真实性的文体特征。(2)在扩展资源中,引发主要通过情态动词、情态附加词和证据表达式来体现。其中 can, would, may 等低值情态动词高频出现,也反映了情态动词的使用与语篇类型有着密切的关系;摘引资源主要通过转述动词,如 confirm, consider 等来体现,这些转述动词的使用具有预示和支配语篇意义的功能,同时也隐性地表达了作者对命题的态度。(3)在紧缩资源中,弃言主要体现为否定词、让步词或某些连接词。在弃言次类别中,否定和对立资源在语料库中呈现均衡分布;在宣言次类别中,同意、宣称和认可次类别呈现显著性差异。其中认可次类别主要通过特定的语法结构来体现。认可次类别的大量使用增强了语篇的多声性和互动性。钱建伟和 Rob Law(2016)以评价理论介入系统为理论框架,从积极话语分析的角度出发,探究《纽约时报》对近几年我国游客的行为及其形象的报道可以发现,西方主流报刊对中国游客的报道不再是围绕以前普遍认为的消极形象,而是通过对相关不文明行为的定义及事实的梳理,借用人际对话空间的压缩或扩展策略,开始转向对中国游客形象的积极建构,从而引导读者做出正面的评价。狄艳华和柳锦(2016)从评价理论的介入视角对美国反恐局发布的反恐语篇进行分析研究发现,反恐语篇中否认资源主要通过具有比较和反对意义的词汇手段实现,包括否定资源和反预期资源,呈现显隐特征和强弱特征。一方面,恐怖分子是对话双方共同的敌人和打击的对象,通过传递这一信息塑造了积极的美国形象,并与听者/读者结成反恐结盟;另一方面,反恐是正义合理的伟大事业,进而提出打击恐怖犯罪的最佳方式是国际合作。美国政府和人民在反恐事业中取得了巨大的成就,他们有信心、有能力与其他国家和组织共同努力,坚决与恐怖分子和恐怖活动做斗争。否认资源的运用将评价理论介入系统融入反恐语篇中,收缩了说者/作者与听者/读者的对话空间,树立了声源的权威性,提高了话语的可信度,避免说者/作者的观点和立场受到强烈的攻击和反驳,排除了可能存在的外部观点和立场,是一种有效的语篇策略。刘婷婷和徐加新(2018)在评价理论介入系统的框架下,以定量分析与定性分析相结合的方法,对比分析《纽约时报》(*The New York Times*)和《华盛顿邮报》(*The Washington Post*),以及《人民日报》和《光明日报》上的英汉政治社论语篇中的介入资源,揭示其分布特征及产生的语篇人际意义的异同。研究发现:(1)英语社论倾向于选择不同类型的多语介入资源,对单语的介入方式选择很少;在多语的体现方式上,倾向于大量使用引入篇外声音的借言和增强语篇对话强度的对话扩展,而在后者的实现方式上使用大量情态值较低的表可能性的情态成分。总体上看,语篇整体呈现的对话性较强。(2)在汉语社论中,对单语的介入方式选择较多,平均只有三分之一的句子使用多语式的介入评价。而在这为数不多的多语介入资源中,更倾向于对自言的选择,通过评论者自己的声音经常由主体性来提高语篇的对话程度;此外,虽然对对话扩展也持较多的选择,但与英语社论选择倾向相似,多数是由表义务、责任的情态成分体现的,这与英语社论有较大的差异。总体上说,较之英语,汉语社论语篇的对话性较弱。

关于态度系统的国外研究,Martin(2000)在"Beyond Exchange:Appraisal Systems in English"一文中指出,态度系统是评价理论的核心部分,它由三个子系统——情感、判断和鉴赏构成。White(2002)认为,态度系统是描述、解释和探究语言使用情况的一种特殊方法,它的用途是评价语言。通过对评价语言的使用,表明人们采取的不同观点和立场,控制人际关系和建构语篇人物的社会角色,如表达说话者/作者的态度和情感反应,通过在文中进行明确的语言描述或间接的暗示,人们就能与和自己持有相同或不同观点的人保持合适的距离。Martin 和 Rose(2002)合著了 *Working with Discourse：Meaning Beyond Clause*,该书详细阐述了评价理论态度系统的框架,并将态度系统应用于对各种不同的体裁分析中,他们指出:"评价是一个概括性术语,包括一切可评估的语言使用,作者/说话者建立自身立场和位置,与真实的或潜在的回应者进行协商。"这在某种程度上扩大了态度系统的使用范围,发展和完善了态度系统。2005 年,评价理论态度系统得到进一步发展,Martin 和 White 的著作 *The Language of Evaluation：Appraisal in English* 深入阐述了评价理论态度系统,使得态度系统的研究系统化和可理解化。自此,评价理论成为一个以态度系统为核心,分析语篇中人际意义和立场的完整评价体系。

评价理论态度系统在不断应用于实践过程中逐渐走向完善。如 Ngo 和 Unsworth(2015)从评价理论的角度分析了越南研究生英语口语中评价资源的部署问题,旨在说明在讨论主题时使用的评价语言范围,并补充了评价理论的态度系统。以态度系统的子系统鉴赏为例,Lee(2015)对澳大利亚本科生撰写的高级论文和低级论文进行了比较,试图找出评价语言的使用是否有助于学术话语的成功。Roux 和 Valladares(2015)运用评价理论分析墨西哥中学教师对该国英语基础教育项目的态度,研究发现教师对该项目的消极态度与他们对该项目中关于教师培训的数量和质量的消极评价相关。Alexanne Don(2016)从评价理论的角度研究了文章"It is hard to mesh all this"中的态度系统,为研究书面语篇中可能引用或用于暗示的态度提供了建议和方法。除教育领域外,评价理论态度系统也被应用于媒体和广告领域。Khoo,Nourbakhsh 和 Na(2012)运用评价理论对网络新闻语篇中的情感表达进行分析。Korenek(2014)对微博内容中关于商品和服务的语料进行评价分析,改进了微博中情感分类的方法。

在国内,许多学者也关注小说语篇和童话语篇的研究,尝试从评价理论态度系统的视角对文学作品做出独特的价值判断,探究提高文学作品鉴赏能力的新途径。尚必武(2008)通过深入分析小说中的态度资源,窥探了小说中主人公的人物情感和性格,并为小说的情感解读提供了新维度,同时也拓展了评价理论态度系统的适用性。管淑红(2011)以弗吉尼亚·伍尔夫的著名小说《达洛卫夫人》为例,探讨了意识流小说叙事的态度系统及其体现以及它们如何推动小说爱情主题的构建。该研究扩展和深化了 Halliday 和 Martin 等功能语言学家基于词汇语法的人际意义研究,把小说的评价意义置于小句层和整个语篇层来阐释。韩颖(2014)从态度和介入系统角度对格林童话的态度资源进行了定性与定量结合的研究,发现格林童话态度资源的分布特点体现了民间童话的语域特征和教育导向。

也有学者把态度系统运用到翻译研究领域。蒋平和王琳琳(2010)运用评价理论的态度系统对《背影》及其两个英译本的态度资源进行了分析比较,尝试从这一角度鉴别译文在有关处理上的优劣。研究发现,评价理论的态度系统有助于鉴别译文态度意义的优劣,但其具体操作还需在翻译义值的取向和语篇整体视角上加以完善。陈梅和文军(2013)对白居易诗歌的英译在态度资源的分布和使用频率方面进行了研究,为诗歌翻译提供了个案数据,也拓展了评价理论态度系统运用的文体范围。李鑫(2016)借助评价理论中的态度系统,以党的十八大报告为案例,探讨了态度系统对政治外宣文本翻译研究的影响和意义。司显柱和庞玉厚(2018)认为,态度系统在源语成功地转换为目标语的过程中起到不可忽视的重要作用,是评判翻译质量的重要参数。

态度系统也为法律语篇和新闻语篇的研究提供了新视角。蒋婷(2016)认为,在仲裁调解过程中,仲裁员所用的态度资源恰当与否关系着调解的成败。态度资源在构建并维系仲裁员与当事人之间的和谐关系、促进调解和表明其态度等方面,都发挥了重要作用。施光(2016,2017)运用评价理论对刑事判决书的态度系统进行了分析,发现数量最多的态度表达是判断,其次是鉴赏,最少的是情感。葛琴(2015)运用态度子系统分析了国际政治事件的中英文对应报道,探讨了汉英政治新闻语篇中人际意义构建的异同,对比了两者在情感、判断、鉴赏三种评价资源上的分布差异,旨在了解其中的评价机制,从而更好地理解政治新闻话语的隐性含义。田华静(2015)以评价理论为依据,分析了外刊新闻报道中的态度资源与身份建构的关系。研究发现,态度资源对新闻语篇中的身份建构和身份平衡起着至关重要的作用。基于评价理论分析框架,陈令君和赵闯(2016)采用定性与定量相结合的方法识别并研究了"中国梦"相关英语新闻语篇中显性和隐性态度资源传递的话语意义。李晓雪和黄滔(2017)借助评价理论的态度和介入系统,从词汇意义层面,对美国主流报纸有关中国阅兵的语篇报道进行了分析,以揭示报道中评价资源的分布特点和差异,由此窥探美国主流报纸在对此活动报道中所体现的态度差异。

从以上综述可见,学者们把介入和态度系统应用于各类语篇分析时,往往先统计各种介入或态度资源在语篇中的使用频率,然后归纳每种介入或态度资源在语篇中对应的词汇类别和特点,结合语篇的语境要素,阐释语篇作者如何使用介入或态度策略实现语篇的交际目的。然而,除了李君和张德禄(2010)以外,很少有学者在分析话语的评价资源时,将语篇结构纳入研究框架。本书认为,在阐释话语策略的人际意义时,应该把语篇结构和评价资源结合起来,通过揭示语篇结构中各个阶段或部分的评价资源分布,能更有效地阐明随着语篇的逐步展开以及各阶段话语内容的变化,作者如何运用或调整介入和态度策略来实现语篇局部和整体的交际目的。因此,对于"一带一路"对外新闻的话语策略研究,本书把新闻语篇结构作为研究重点之一。

二、修辞功能的研究

在国外,一般认为修辞学的研究最早源于公元前 5 世纪的古希腊,具体指"公众演讲的公民技艺"。在传统上,它一直被等同于"言说的技艺"或者"说服的技艺"(刘亚猛,2008)。在最早孕育修辞学的古希腊社会中,演讲与民众事物是息息相关的,在出现民事、政治争端和思想冲突时,劝说性的演讲就会起到关键性作用。由于演讲在当时的社会生活中所起的重要作用以及演讲本身所具有的技巧,越来越多的人开始从各种演讲题材中选出那些被认为具有劝说作用的成分,并对这些成分进行分门别类地归纳、总结,最终形成了一门专门研究劝说性艺术的学科——修辞学。

作为古希腊修辞学的集大成者,亚里士多德(Aristotle)首次使修辞学系统化为一个统一的理论体系,被认为是西方古典修辞学的创始人。美国修辞学者 Schwartz(1966)认为,"自亚里士多德时代,经过 19 世纪至今的大多数修辞学著作,其方法和内容与亚里士多德的修辞学都有某些相似性"。Corbett(1999)更是大胆宣称,现代西方修辞学就其精华而言仍然是两千多年前亚里士多德的东西。

西方修辞学的发展经历了古希腊罗马时期、中世纪时期、文艺复兴时期、启蒙运动时期和 20 世纪时期。近代古典修辞学整体呈现出三大研究趋势：认知论的、纯文学的和演说术。这一时期的代表人物有 George Campbell 和 Hugh Blair。Campbell（1963）融合了亚里士多德（Aristotle）、西塞罗（Cicero）、昆体良（Quintilian）的修辞思想，结合功能心理学和经验主义，提出了科学修辞学的思想，试图了解修辞与思维的关系，把修辞学建立在研究人类本质的基础之上，并提出了"听众中心论"的修辞观点。他说修辞是"人性的科学"，通过"提供信息、说服、愉悦、感动的方式作用于听众的灵魂"，认为修辞的目的是"启迪理解，满足想象，触动情感或影响意志"。作为纯文学运动的代表人物，Blair（2015）的修辞理论主要涉及修辞学、文学与批评之间的关系，除了纯文学的论述外，还讨论了审美情趣、语法、文体风格、演说词等。

在国内，中国的古典修辞学可追溯到先秦时期，该时期的修辞学可称作是"游说"与"辩论"的学说。现代"修辞学"演变发展成语言学的一门学科，属于语用学的一种，其研究的内容是提高语言表达效果的规律。自西方古典修辞学被引进中国，国内大多数学者从司法调解的角度对其修辞功能进行了解读，如程朝阳（2014）曾分析亚里士多德的古典修辞学理论，发现其三种说服功能可以被调解人用来帮助矛盾双方转变他们的思想框架，重新定位冲突，以达成双方都满意的纠纷解决方案。李静涵和韩晋（2017）认为，修辞学源于法庭论辩和政治演说的需求，传统的修辞学是一门说服的艺术，与语言学关系密切，是获得法庭论辩胜利的重要手段。除此之外，学者们也运用修辞功能这一理论进行跨学科的应用。这些应用涉及社会生活的诸多方面，集中于话语分析、公众演讲以及教育教学领域等。例如，樊明明（1999）对比分析了中西古典修辞学中说服活动的三种修辞功能，试图说明话语权力在两种文化中的结构和功能。鞠玉梅（2013）借助亚里士多德的古典修辞理论，从修辞劝说的角度探讨了元话语的使用，分析元话语是如何在学术论文语篇中实现古典修辞学中的情感说服、人品说服、和逻辑说服。聂薇（2017）运用亚里士多德修辞理论研究了英语演讲语料，分析了演讲者如何利用这三种修辞手段构建国家形象。白文昌（2018）以亚里士多德在《修辞学》中提出的三种说服功能为理论依据，分析了说服三原则对课堂教学的启迪意义。研究发现，良好的课堂教学离不开三个要素，即教师要善于运用自身的人格魅力，调动学生的情感，合理利用与教学内容关联的论证技巧。

然而，将评价理论与古典修辞理论相结合来研究态度修辞功能的却不多见。彭宣维（2012）曾以评价理论为着眼点，系统考察了亚里士多德著述中体现的评价思想，发现两者涉及的主要范畴之间有实质性的渊源关系，唯各自的出发点有别。他还指出，态度子系统的情感资源与修辞学相关，是关于"修辞性劝说"的演说目的和效果。

本书将结合评价理论态度系统和古典修辞理论，通过定量统计和定性分析、论证态度资源与修辞功能的相互联系，试图揭示态度韵律如何实现三大修辞功能。

三、新闻结构的研究

新闻,是指报纸、电台、电视台、互联网等媒体经常使用的记录与传播信息的一种文体,是记录社会、传播信息、反映时代的一种文体。新闻是反映新发生的、重要的、有意义的、能引起广泛兴趣的事实,具有迅速、明了、简短的特点,是一种最有效的宣传形式。新闻的结构分为内部结构和外部结构。内部结构是指新闻内容的组织与构选,包括标题、导语、主体、背景和结语五个部分。外部结构是指新闻外在的形态和基本格局,是作者的构思、新闻作品的内容得以展开而体现的整体形态。它根据不同的新闻事实采用不同的反映形式,主要有四种形式:倒金字塔式结构、时间顺序式结构、悬念式结构、并列式结构。

在国外,不少学者对新闻话语的体裁进行了研究。例如,Van Leeuwen(1987)将系统功能语言学中的语类理论应用到新闻文本研究,阐述了新闻文本的不同阶段是如何产生各种语类功能,从而实现不同的修辞目标。Van Dijk(1988)将认知研究应用到新闻结构中去,用"新闻图式(News Schemata)"这个术语来解释新闻结构。该结构主要展现新闻故事的主题结构(thematic structure),是分析新闻语篇的核心框架,它有两个主体部分:总括(summary)和故事(story)。总括包含标题(headline)与导语(lead),而故事包括情景(situation)与评议(comments)。图式结构通过一个从上至下的等级顺序(hierarchical order)清晰展现新闻语篇的宏观形式与内容,体现所包含话题(themes/topics)的整体组织结构。标题与导语反映全文的中心话题,情景是支撑中心话题的细节描述,评议则是记者的看法与观点。Fairclough(1995)认为 Van Dijk 的图式结构反映了绝大多数新闻语篇的篇章结构,因此,他将此结构称为"整体框架"(generic structure)。他将图式结构中的情景与评议更名为附属部分(satellites)和综合报道(wrap-up),其中附属部分是具体描述新闻事件的各个段落,综合报道是结局。他认为,图式结构中四个部分出现的顺序是固定的,如导语不可能在标题之前等,但构成附属部分各段落的顺序可以调整。图式主题结构中的每一成分通常能在宏观语义结构中找到与之相对应的部分,如图式主题结构中新闻标题就能与宏观语义结构中的全文主题相对应。Bell(1998)认为新闻故事框架可简化为特定属性(attribution)、概要(abstract)、故事(the story proper)三大部分。特定属性主要指新闻故事的来源(包括记者的姓名、报道时间、地点等);概要主要包括标题及导语,起到新闻简介的作用;而故事本身则由一个或多个情节(episode)构成,每个情节之中又包含若干个小的事件(event),是对新闻报道的细节描述。有时还涉及三个补充成分:背景(background)、评论(commentary)和追踪报道(follow-up)。背景主要介绍在此新闻事件发生之前的事情;评论则是记者对目前事件的观察与反映,以达到帮助读者理解的目的;追踪报道是指报道一个事件主要行为(action)之后出现的别的行为。Bell 的新闻故事宏观结构更侧重于报刊新闻报道的结构特点,而对新闻语体的研究有所忽视。White(1998)从词汇语法和语义学的角度提出了环绕轨道模型这一新闻语类结构,注重新闻话语的修辞功能。他将新闻语篇按语义关系分为五部分:开篇、详述、解释、评论和背景。

在国内,学者们从不同的角度对新闻结构进行了研究。例如,高山和刘智信(1999)指出,新闻结构的内涵主要包括线索、层次和剪裁三个方面:一篇好新闻,应该是新闻的线索材料、层次结构和裁剪设计相结合的产物。赵福利(2001)对新闻导语的语步结构进行了研究,认为电视新闻导语以特定的语步结构来实现其特定的交际目的。谭姗燕(2005)以认知语言学的经验观、突出观和注意观为基础,分析解读了报刊新闻外部结构的三种主要特征,把认知语言学的观点运用到了与人们日常生活相关的新闻业。王宗炎(2009)对报刊标题语言进行了研究,认为一个好的标题,应能准确概括、生动表达、富有回味,从而起到画龙点睛、加深读者印象的作用,因此,精心构思标题是十分重要的。李锡春(2009)认为,新闻结构分为狭义和广义两种,广义新闻结构对于整个社会宏观状况而言是其新闻实务与新闻属性的引导与新闻阵地的布局,对于具体的微观新闻操作而言则是媒体定位形式、新闻属性和形态的分层与谋划;他认为广义新闻结构的定位由三个因素决定:

读者的分层性、阅读习惯和社会发展动态。华进(2013)指出了网络新闻的结构和原则,明确网络新闻文本是在何种结构原则的规范下以何种结构模式来叙事,丰富了新闻的叙事手法,为网络新闻改革提供了借鉴。范红(2002)认为,虽然宏观结构是一个强有力的新闻语篇分析的综合框架,但它有一定的局限。首先,此框架的焦点集中在语篇的呈现方式(representations),忽视了新闻报道应反映的各种社会关系与社会身份(identities)等深层次问题,在某种程度上脱离社会文化的大环境。其次,对新闻语篇的分析仅局限于语言分析,片面强调新闻语篇结构的统一性、固定性,禁锢了新闻创作的多样性与异类性。在确定微观结构时,作者也不能超越其词句选择的范围,否则其新闻报道的真实性将会贬值,读者便会被误导。因此,进行新闻语篇分析时,必须将语篇的宏观结构与微观结构相结合,还应考虑诸多的社会因素。杨洸和郭中实(2016)指出,传统的新闻呈现方式以倒金字塔为主,安排上依照事件的重要性依次递减:将最重要的事实放置在新闻开头,接下来是次重要的内容,事件的背景信息经常放在新闻的末尾。因此,受众一般只要看到新闻开头就知晓事件的最新进展,排在后面的信息可能会被漫不经心地处理,甚至中断阅读,无法维持受众的注意力,无法使缺少相关背景知识的受众了解事件,导致了较低程度的新闻理解,尤其是不准确的新闻记忆。相比之下,叙事性新闻结构是另一种常见的新闻写作方式——通俗地说,也叫"说书"形式(storytelling)。叙事性新闻结构与写小说类似,通常将报道事件按照时间发展顺序依次展开,聚焦新闻的主人公,描述主人公的行动和经历,突出个人特点,并且从受众的角度采写新闻,制造悬念,将受众的注意力从事件开始持续到新闻结尾,使得受众对事件的原貌有清晰了解。实证研究发现,叙事性结构比倒金字塔结构更容易重新唤起受众的记忆,产生丰富的新闻理解。

综观国内外相关文献,在新闻传播学领域,大多数学者认为新闻语篇结构以"倒金字塔形"为主(MacDougall,1982;Schudson,1982;Mencher,2010)。在语言学领域,有学者提出了不同看法,认为新闻报道的结构经常以标题和导语作为语义中心,其他内容环绕该中心,策略性地分布在语篇内(White,1997;White,1998;White,2000)。此观点的核心就是,新闻作者把新闻事件中最重要的元素放在语篇开头——当然,在选择新闻元素、评判其重要性时,作者必然把自己的观点立场渗透在语篇中。我们随后的研究将表明,虽然有些"一带一路"对外新闻语篇结构类似"倒金字塔形",但是大多数"一带一路"对外新闻并非如此,它们更符合"环绕标题/导语形":以标题和导语开启语篇,作为语篇的语义核心,其他内容环绕在此核心周围,从语义上与其遥相呼应。

四、"一带一路"新闻语篇的研究

2013 年 9 月和 10 月,中国国家主席习近平在出访中亚和东南亚国家期间，先后提出共建"丝绸之路经济带"和"21世纪海上丝绸之路"的重大倡议，得到国际社会高度关注。自该倡议提出以来，国内外媒体对此进行了广泛深入的报道，相关学者对"一带一路"新闻语篇的研究也与日俱增，主要集中在新闻传播学和语言学领域。

在新闻传播领域，阮宗泽（2014）分析了"一带一路"倡议对外宣传的现状，从外交与安全层面探讨了中国崛起过程中周边环境的变革及潜在影响，提出建设"一带一路"发展周边外交是构建我国和平发展的新途径。张允和朱卉（2015）对百度指数下多媒体平台"一带一路"报道的政策性新闻受众关注度进行了分析，研究了受众在面对国家主流媒体和核心区主流媒体报道同一政策信息的媒介路径的偏好与选择。廖杨标（2015）选取2014全年《人民日报》海外版"一带一路"新闻报道的内容进行了研究，通过量化分析，总结《人民日报》在对外经济新闻报道中使用的框架，以窥我国在对外经济报道中的现状与不足。夏春平（2015）通过对中新社的"一带一路"相关报道进行分析，主要通过对该社举办的"丝绸之路华媒万里行"大型采访报道活动的梳理和总结，为今后的报道提供思路。周凯（2015）从传播学视角研究了"一带一路"建设在对外传播时面临的困境并提出了对策。程果（2015）从新闻议程设置视角探讨了如何为"一带一路"倡议进行国际舆论宣传。郑华和李婧（2016）选取了美国《纽约时报》和《华盛顿邮报》中"一带一路"相关报道作为研究文本，从语境创设、语言标识符运用、消息来源及倾向性三个维度探讨了作为一种精英话语的美国媒介话语对于中国"一带一路"倡议的认知。研究发现,美国对于"一带一路"倡议的看法具有复杂性,积极、中性、消极观点并存。这反映了美国的矛盾心理:美国一方面需要稳定发展的中国,另一方面又担心中国的发展会打破现有国际格局。孙有中和江璐(2017)以澳大利亚四家主流新闻媒体作为考察对象的研究发现,澳大利亚的"一带一路"报道总量较少,但呈上升趋势;报道强度与中国政府"一带一路"政策阐释、推广、双边外交和经贸活动强度成正相关;报道信源在行业间分布相对均衡,但过度依赖欧美西方智库和发言人;"一带一路"倡议主要出现在经济和政治议题报道中:经济报道更为正面,认为"一带一路"倡议将为澳大利亚和沿线国家带来利益,政治报道关注中国崛起可能带来的地缘政治变局及对现有国际秩序的"威胁"。毛伟(2018)通过量化分析和内容分析,对新华社在拉美地区传播"一带一路"倡议的现状与效果进行了研究。研究发现,新华社针对拉美地区发布的"一带一路"新闻报道数量较多,报道主题相对集中于政治和经济领域,但拉美当地媒体转引量不足。张莉和陆洪磊(2018)以发源于英国的不同市场定位的五种媒体关于"一带一路"的报道为分析对象,对国际新闻生产的全球化和本土化论争进行了新的辩证思考,并探讨了国际传播中影响我国"一带一路"倡议报道的因素。研究发现,全球化和本土化因素在海外媒体关于"一带一路"新闻生产的不同环节产生了不同的影响,而且在"一带一路"国际议题的新闻生产中,媒体市场的区域定位比媒体市场的阶层定位影响更显著。李雪威和赵连雪(2018)发现,日本主流报刊媒体对"一带一路"倡议的报道呈现出一个动态变化的过程,报道量和报道强度指数总体呈上升趋势;对"一带一路"报道的态度经历了初期消极抵触、中期犹疑观望、近期积极合作的转变;对"一带一路"报道的关注焦点从具体金融领域的亚洲基础设施投资银行(亚投行)转向作为顶层设计的"一带一路",重点关注与中国开展合作的国家与地区,同时也关注具体合作领域的进展情况。安珊珊和梁馨月(2018)以美国主流媒体对"一带一路"国际合作高峰论坛的相关报道为研究对象,围绕新闻显性要素构成与隐性框架结构两个向度,探讨了美国主流媒体如何构建"一带一路"新闻报道框架,并进一步检验了美国媒体建构中国国家形象之媒体偏见的稳定性。研究发现,美国媒体依然延续强势国家立场,对"一带一路"倡议的报道颇多臆断解读;美国新闻报道框架既强调中国的重要性,也保有风险认知与威胁警惕。

在语言学领域,朱桂生和黄建滨(2016)采用批评性话语分析的方法,以美国《华盛顿邮报》的相关报道作为分析对象,从文本、话语实践和社会实践三个层面探讨了美国主流媒体如何建构中国的"一带一路"形象、建构了怎样的"一带一路"形象以及这些形象建构的背后存在怎样的社会意识形态等问题。研究发现,《华盛顿邮报》通过分类、及物性、文本架构、互文性等手段,将中国的"一带一路"塑造成一种殖民扩张、将中国塑造成重利轻义的霸权形象。这种形象塑造的背后与美国社会存在的"中国威胁论"密切相关。赵雅莹、郭继荣和车向前(2016)从评价理论中态度系统的视角分析了英国主流媒体关于"一带一路"报道中使用的态度词褒贬含义及其所属类别,用可视化数据量化的方式解读了英国对此倡议的态度,为"一带一路"后续宣传策略的制定提供了参考,展现了一种情报解读的量化分析思路。单理扬(2017)从隐喻情节概念视角,分析了美国主流报刊对"一带一路"倡议的报道。研究发现,语料中的隐喻叙事放大了中美间的利益之争,容易激活并强化读者脑海中的零和博弈概念,令读者对中美关系的未来产生一种迷思,即认为两者之间只能有一个赢家,较少存在合作及共赢的可能性。这显示美国主流报刊仍未完全接受中国所提出的新型大国关系,仍存在诉诸历史、选择对立的倾向。董希骁(2018)基于系统功能语言学理论,从新闻标题中各类及物性过程的参与者入手,探究了罗马尼亚媒体在报道"一带一路"时的态度差异及其原因。研究发现,从数量上看,正面和中性报道占绝大部分,这与"一带一路"倡议下中罗关系的走向是相符的,虽然一些媒体有时出现不和谐的声音,但绝大多数质疑并非"原发性"的,缺乏来自本土的论据支撑,相关报道的标题中难觅罗马尼亚的影子,很多反对之声都是拾西方媒体之牙慧,少数还是罗马尼亚国内政治斗争的结果;研究还针对目前我国对罗马尼亚的"一带一路"建设宣传工作提出了建议。蒋岳春(2018)通过分析《华盛顿邮报》关于中国"一带一路"倡议的相关报道,探究了该报如何表征"一带一路"及通过何种修辞手法形成该表征。研究发现,《华盛顿邮报》将"一带一路"表征为带有扩张意图的"中国版马歇尔计划"和"掠夺渠道",中国被歪曲为"钻营者"。为形成该表征,该报采用以对比为主的修辞手法,突显"一带一路"引发的相关国家利益和价值等冲突,将读者的注意力引向"一带一路"的负面影响。该报的这种表征源于中美利益观和意识形态方面的差异。唐青叶和史晓云(2018)基于新闻语料库,对比分析了《纽约时报》《印度时报》和《欧盟报》有关"一带一路"的报道,考察了这些媒体对"一带一路"话语建构的差异、情感态度的变化及其原因。研究发现,《纽约时报》通过对其他国家隐性评价表达美国的反对立场,体现了"重大机遇""害怕失去霸主地位""机遇""威胁"的暧昧态度;《印度时报》对"一带一路"认知经历了印度"不情愿加入""有可能获益""仍然谨慎观望"三个阶段;《欧盟报》经历了从总体支持、到欧盟各国争相加入、再到支持态度逐渐具体化的转变。邵颖(2018)运用系统功能语言学中概念功能的及物性理论,分析了马来西亚总理纳吉布的署名文章。研究发现,从内容选择、形式组织到话语策略的运用,纳吉布成功地实现了发表此次署名文章所要达到的目的:(1)正面评价"一带一路"倡议的积极意义,进一步加强与中国的关系;(2)强调马来西亚在"一带一路"中获得的实实在在的利益,正面回击国内反对势力的抨击和质疑,争取民众支持;(3)树立马来西亚的典范形象,表达开创"亚洲世纪"的雄心壮志。张虹(2018)从系统功能语言学及物性系统视角对南非媒体"一带一路"倡议报道进行了分析。研究发现,南非新闻媒体对"一带一路"倡议的报道是正面的,认为"一带一路"倡议是"全球经济政治秩序的顺风车""事关各国生死存亡的举措""推动全球经济发展的方案",进而构建出中国作为"全球治理掌舵者"的国家形象。邵斌、蔡颖莹和余晓燕(2018)基于语料库,考察了西方媒体对"一带一路"的总体态度,借助聚类分析手段探索了西方各国对其评价的差异,采用主题词分析呈现了英国、美国、德国、澳大利亚和新西兰等五国对其关注的焦点。研究发现:(1)误读和"中国威胁论"的消极声音虽时有存在,但西方媒体对"一带一路"的总体态度是肯定的;(2)美、加等北美国家某些媒体对"一带一路"有消极评价,而沿线国家,特别是中东欧国家,多为积极评价;(3)西方各国媒体对"一带一路"的关注焦点不同,主要是出于国家利益、经济利益以及意识形态的考量。何伟和高然(2018)基于系统功能语言学及物性系统理论,以《新西兰先驱报》为例,对新西兰主流媒体有关中国"一带一路"倡议的报道进行了分析。研究发现,新西兰主流媒体主要通过动作、关系、心理、交流、影响过程,并通过赋予"中国""一带一路"等施事、载体或标记、认知者或情感表现者、交流方等角色,以及赋予"新西兰"施事、受事、意愿表现者、交流方等角色,将中国及"一带一路"倡议看作具有高度能动性的主体,将新西兰既看作一个受影响的客体,又看作一个发挥能动作用的主体。辛斌和吴玲莉(2018)分析了中美媒体有关"一带一路"倡议的报道中介入资源的分布情况,发现中美都更多地调用了"对话性扩展"资源,表明双方在表达自己立场态度的同时,都愿意为不同的观点预留对话空间。聂薇(2018)以英国主流媒体英国广播公司(BBC)作为考察对象,从系统功能语言学及物性视角对其有关"一带一路"倡议的报道进行了较为系统的表征分析。研究发现,英国主流媒体对该倡议充满矛盾与纠结,既兴奋于与中国的巨大贸易利益,又担心中国的崛起引起地缘政治变局,以历时视角分析英国渐进显现的"充满疑虑—疑虑接纳—欢迎支持"三个阶段的态度变化及原因。钟馨(2018)采用批评话语分析范式,基于语料库批评话语分析法,探讨了英国全国性报纸中"一带一路"话语的意义建构问题。研究发现:(1)英国全国性报纸频繁用解释逻辑的目的语义关系,建构了"一带一路"倡议的目的意义,即中国谋求在亚欧非乃至全球范围的经济政治影响力;(2)主要用正面的述语策略,借助大量褒义的谓语、定语、明喻、暗喻、搭配等语言形式,建构了英国对于"一带一路"积极肯定、乐于参与的态度,同时也多次借助贬义的谓语,建构了中国投资英国重要的基础设施会威胁英国国家安全的负面意义;(3)用突显"中巴经济走廊"建设的系列精确数据的语言形式,建构了巴基斯坦正在积极参与"一带一路"建设的态度;(4)主要用对比语义关系的修辞惯用句式,建构了印度对于"一带一路"戒备抵制的消极态度。汪波(2018)选取韩国三大报刊当中与"一带一路"倡议高度相关的97篇新闻报道为研究对象,对这些报道中所反映的韩国对于"一带一路"倡议的认识和态度进行了分析。研究发现,根据报道频次及韩国政治背景的变化,韩媒对"一带一路"的态度大致可以分为三个阶段:第一个阶段为热议期,主要关注"一带一路"的性质及合作方式;第二个阶段为冷淡期,不再关心韩国与"一带一路"的关系;第三个阶段为焦虑期,重点关注"一带一路"背景下中国与各国的关系。江潇潇(2018)以态度系统为理论框架,分析了斯里兰卡主流媒体对"一带一路"的相关报道。研究发现,该国媒体大量使用情感、裁决、鉴赏三种态度资源对"一带一路"进行评价,认为"一带一路"倡议既是全球经济助推器,也是斯里兰卡强国之路上的机遇与助力,同时认为斯里兰卡在积极参与该倡议的同时应把握好发展节奏。

综上所述,新闻传播学领域的学者,主要从新闻议程设置、报道框架和传播效果等视角,研究中外媒体"一带一路"相关报道,同时结合外交、文化、历史、政治和经济因素,论述"一带一路"对中国和国际社会发展、变革的深刻含义。虽然此类研究揭示了"一带一路"新闻的报道立场、宣传策略、语篇特征和意义影响,但研究的视角较为宏观,忽略了新闻语篇中话语互动、对话协商的语言人际意义。而语言学领域的学者,主要基于系统功能语言学理论,从批评话语分析视角,对国外媒体"一带一路"新闻语篇进行文本研究,但是,目前鲜有学者从语言学角度研究中国媒体关于"一带一路"的对外新闻话语,分析字里行间新闻作者渗透的观点和立场。

　　本研究以评价理论和古典修辞理论为理论框架,以White(1998)的新闻结构模型为基础,分析中国媒体的英语对外新闻话语,探究此类语篇结构中各部分的介入和态度资源分布规律、语篇的韵律话语模式、修辞说服功能和人际意义。

第三章　理论框架

本章主要介绍评价理论的介入系统和态度系统，修辞功能和新闻结构模型，为本研究奠定坚实的理论基础。

一、评价理论概述

Martin 等人创立的评价理论是系统功能语言学在研究人际意义基础上发展起来的新的词汇—语法框架，是对 Halliday 人际意义研究的新发展。它关注"语篇中所协商的各种态度、所涉及情感的强度以及表明价值和联盟读者的各种方式"。评价理论旨在阐释发话人如何利用语言资源来传递对事态的观点和立场，以此来拉拢相同观点和疏远不同观点。Martin 和 White(2005)将评价理论分成三大系统：态度、介入和级差。态度是指心理受到影响后对人类行为、文本/过程及现象做出的判断和鉴赏，态度资源可进一步分为情感、判断和鉴赏三个次系统。介入系统是用来衡量作者声音与语篇所表达命题的关系，指语言使用者利用介入手段调节对所说或所写的内容承担的相应责任和义务，主要包括自言和借言两个子系统。级差系统是对态度、介入程度的分级资源,即对语言强度或清晰度的加强或减弱,包括语势和聚焦两个子系统。态度是评价系统的中心枢纽,介入和级差均围绕中心系统展开,其中,介入系统被看作是态度的源泉,作者运用介入策略来凸显语篇的评价立场与人际意义。

二、介入系统和态度系统

介入系统是在 Bakhtin 的对话性和 Kristeva 的互文性基础上发展而来的。Bakhtin(1981)指出,所有的话语都是彼此关联的,话语具有内在的对话性,任何一个具体的话语都是特定领域中的言语交际链条上的一环,言语交际是多方面积极的"思想交流"过程,它们彼此熟悉,相互反应,揭示了之前言语的影响或者提到了之前言语的内容,与此同时,期待实际或潜在交际对象的反应。后来,语言学家 Kristeva(1986)发展了 Bakhtin 的对话理论,她认为,所有语篇都是由引语整合而成的,每个语篇都是吸收和转换其他语篇的结果,因此任何语篇本质上都具有互文性。Martin(2005)把语言对话性和语篇的互文性引入了介入系统,认为交际者运用语言介入系统,协商和调整语篇内外各种声音之间的潜势。介入系统关注的是评价者参与话语的方式和程度,是评价客体与主体间相互照应、唤起或协商彼此社会地位的语言资源,具有主体间性的特征。主体间性是构建语篇意义的核心范畴,在主体间性的基础上,作者通过运用介入资源,直接或间接地引用他人话语,表明自己对语篇中话语蕴含的价值观念所持的态度(支持、反对、中立、不置可否),以及期待交际对象对此做出某种反应(赞同、犹豫、怀疑、排斥),从而使对话成为可能。

由此可见,介入是实现对主体间性进行调控的语言策略,作者既可以直接表达评价,也可以邀请他人的声音进来给予间接评价,加强评价效果。这两种方式分别被称为单声(自言)和多声(借言)模式。单声是评价活动只通过作者单个人的声音实施的,说话者以自圆其说的方式陈述其立场或观点,并承担相应的责任,在话语信息传递的语言中不涉及其他任何其他声音的介入。多声指作者以开放式的风格陈述其立场或观点,并以多种方式把其他声音投射到语篇中而展开对事物的陈述。

Martin 和 White(2005)认为,如果从对话性的角度来说,单声也是有立场的,只是它似乎只提供了一种立场,没有公开其他立场的存在。多声是明确表示可能存在另一种意见的言语,主要包括两种介入策略:对话收缩和对话扩展。对话收缩是指语篇引用多种声音后对其中的某些声音进行限制,以缩小对话空间。对话收缩包括否认策略和公告策略。否认策略是说明自己不同意,直接排斥或驳斥某观点,以压缩协商空间,经常通过"不是、没有"等否定词汇或者"虽然、但是"等转折词汇来体现。公告策略是明确支持某观点,压制其他意见,以紧缩对话空间,经常通过"显然、毫无疑问、当然"等词汇来体现。对话扩展是指说话人在表达自己的观点、立场和态度时能容纳和接受,甚至鼓励对话人表述与自己不同的观点、态度和立场。对话扩展包括接纳策略和归属策略。接纳策略暗含说话者的声音仅仅是众多可能性、不确定性声音的一种,也可能存在其他不同意见,经常通过"也许、应该、我认为"等词汇来体现。归属策略是把一种意见归属于一种外在主体,是对别人话语的转述,承认这只是很多可能意见之一,从而扩大对话协商空间,常通过"说、声称、表示"等词汇来体现。本研究的介入系统框架如图 3-1(a)所示。

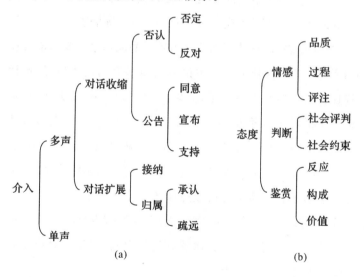

图 3-1　介入系统和态度系统

态度系统如图 3-1(b)所示,分为三个子系统:情感系统、判断系统和鉴赏系统。其中情感是对人们积极或消极情感的研究,是情绪性的,是对行为做出的反应,这种情感反应是人类天生具有的;判断是对人们的行为所持的态度,是伦理性的,是对所做行为的评估;鉴赏是对存在的现象的价值评估,是美学性的,是对现象的评估。情感处于三者的中心,判断和鉴赏是体制化的情感。判断是对"建议"中感情的再加工,即我们应如何做出恰当的行为,其中一些建议已被宗教或国家法律规定为规章制度;鉴赏是对"命题"中感情的再加工,即我们对事物的价值观,其中一些已被定为奖赏制度。

情感属心理学的反应范畴,是人们对行为、文本/过程、现象等的积极或消极反应。Halliday(2004)将情感分为三种类型:品质情感、过程情感和评注情感。品质情感主要指语言使用者通过表示品质的副词短语或品质形容词表达情感,包括描述参与者的情感状态、附加参与者的情绪和过程方式;过程情感指语言使用者运用心理过程小句和行为过程小句等表达感情;评注情感指语言使用者通过情态附加语所表达的情感。

Martin 等人在对情感系统进行分类前提出两个概念:情绪者和触发物。情绪者指经历情绪变化的有意识的参与者,触发物指激发某种情绪的现象(Martin & White, 2005)。虽然还未弄清从词汇角度为情感分类的原则,但他们对情感分类提出以下六个考察因素:

(1)该情感在某一特定文化中通常是积极情感还是消极情感。

(2)情感的实现是否伴随副语言,是否只是以一种内在的情绪状态或心理过程来实现。从语法角度讲，这些区别是行为过程、心理过程和关系过程之间的区别。

（3）该情感是由具体的某一触发物实现还是一种在通常情况下人们所具有的情感。语法上来说，这是心理过程和关系过程的对立。

（4）该情感是如何分成低中高三个等级的。

（5）该情感是否与非真实的意图和刺激有关。从语法角度讲，这种区别是意愿型心理过程与情绪型心理过程之间的区别。

（6）情感分类的三组变量：高兴/不高兴、安全/不安全、满意/不满意。

判断系统属伦理范畴，是指判断者根据一定的社会规范或伦理道德，对人的行为及性格等方面的肯定或否定的评价。Martin 和 White（2005）认为，判断可以分成两类：社会评判和社会约束。社会评判是从规范、才能、坚韧三个角度对人的个性及行为做出的判断：判断一个人的行为是否符合常规，他是否有才干、是否坚强。这种判断往往是口头的，没有书面条文可依。对这些问题是否有同感是组成家庭、结成盟友时要考虑的一个重要方面。社会约束则是从真实和得体两个角度对人的个性及行为做出判断：判断一个人是否坦诚，行为是否妥当。这种判断往往有国家或教廷的已形成法律制度的书面条文可依，共享的价值观是文明社会或宗教教义的基础。如果不遵守这些社会约束，将会受到相应处罚或惩罚。

鉴赏系统属美学范畴,是将事物和自然现象作为评价对象,并从美学角度对它们进行评估,同样有正面含义和负面含义。从总体上来说,对事物的鉴赏可以从三个角度入手:人们对事物的反应,即该事物是否能够吸引我们、是否能够让我们开心;该事物的构成,即评估该事物的均衡性和复杂性;该事物的价值,即评估该事物的创新性、真实性和及时性。由此得出鉴赏系统的三个子系统:反应、构成和价值。Eggins(2004)从语法角度指出,反应、构成、价值对应心理过程的三个分类:反应对应感情,构成对应感知,价值对应认知。从元功能的角度看,Martin 和 White(2005)认为,反应是人际意义取向的,构成是篇章意义取向的,价值则是概念意义取向的。

三、修辞功能

古典修辞学是关于说服的艺术,在 *The Art of Rhetoric* 一书中,Aristotle(1991)指出,修辞是"一种在任何事件上找到可用的说服方法的能力",其中"任何一个事件"是指修辞提供的劝说理论适合于任何领域,可以是劝说听众接受某项政策,也可以是劝说听众接受某一科学原理或者文学艺术原理等;所谓"说服方法",是指言之有理、合乎逻辑的论证方法。他将说服手段分为"非人工"和"人工"两种。所谓"非人工"手段指的是那些先已存在,修辞者无从用其心计的证据,如法定的证人、合法的证言以及白纸黑字的合同等。"人工"说服手段则并非事先存在,而是通过一定方法由修辞者产生的。用亚里士多德自己的话说,"前面的那一类现成就可以用,后面这一类却是发明出来的"。修辞学感兴趣并加以系统研究的只包括后面这一类,即"人工"说服手段。"人工"说服手段可以再细分为三小类:情感说服(pathos)、人品说服(ethos)和逻辑说服(logos)(刘亚猛,2008)。

单理扬(2017)研究美国媒体对"一带一路"倡议的新闻话语时指出,语篇激发读者情绪,使其产生共鸣,促使受众认同文本,最终实现劝说的修辞作用。Aristotle(1991)认为,实现修辞功能的方式有三种:情感说服、人品说服和逻辑说服。情感说服通过调控读者心理和感情,唤起读者情感共鸣,以情动人,说服读者认同语篇立场。当情感说服激起观众的同情等感情时,这些感情使观众接受修辞者的观点及主张或要求采取行动的呼吁。人品说服通过树立说话人道德品质,用人格魅力赢得信任和敬佩,以德服人,影响读者阅读立场。为了实现人品说服,说话者必须展示自己的品德、才智、判断力和善意。当人们认为说话者是值得信任的时候,他们就会接受他的观点。逻辑说服通过篇章组织和逻辑推理,摆事实讲道理,以理服人,引导读者接受作者观点。它是一种借助论据本身说服听众的方式,是通过结构化的论证和逻辑上一致的证据使听众与当事人的意见达成一致。其中,"演说者的品格具有最重要的说服力量"。比起逻辑说服或情感说服,德性更为重要。亚里士多德重视真诚、公正的德性,因为说服者首先要诚实,要通过摆事实、讲道理,通过"每件事本身包含的说服因素"(whatever is persuasive in each case),以确立"真实或显然真实的情况"(the truth or the apparent truth),这样才最有说服力(王妍,2019)。

四、新闻结构模型

White(1998)从词汇语法和语义学的角度提出了环绕轨道模型这一新闻语类结构,该结构注重新闻话语的修辞功能。他将新闻语篇按语义关系分为五部分:开篇、详述、解释、评论和背景。开篇部分由标题和导语构成,包括新闻语篇的核心语义,也是语篇核心人际意义的体现,旨在点明新闻主旨、吸引读者兴趣,为语篇随后各部分展开奠定评价立场。详述部分是针对开篇部分进行具体描述,包括重述和举例两个部分。其中,重述是对开篇中的新闻元素进行扩展和补充,读者通过阅读重述,加深了对开篇中新闻要素的印象和理解,是新闻结构的必要成分。举例是新闻作者通过例子来扩展开篇要素,使得详述部分更具体,更丰富,是新闻结构的可选成分,新闻作者在详述部分通过重述新闻事件和举例解释,力图向读者更全面客观地还原新闻事件。解释部分为开篇部分中的要点描述缘由、目的和结果,旨在展现新闻事件的前因后果,增强新闻报道的逻辑性。评论部分对开篇部分中新闻事件的社会意义、情感影响等进行点评,分为评论事件和评论人物两个部分,旨在表明新闻事件的社会影响,影响读者的评价姿态。背景部分为开篇部分中新闻要素提供背景材料,分为对比同类事件和回顾事件进程两部分,旨在通过历史背景,呈现新闻事件的发展面貌。

White(1998)认为,开篇部分是新闻语篇的核心,具有总结性的功能,而且更重要的是,总结本质上是一种解释性和评价性的过程,其中主体间的定位决定新闻故事的哪些特定要素被视为最重要的信息,从而突显新闻故事的本质或要点。White 的新闻结构模型,结合人际关系理论,旨在识别新闻语篇中某些具有人际意义和语篇意义的结构组织模式以及新闻语篇的构建对新闻作者和读者的评价态度的影响——新闻作者从新闻语篇的字里行间中传达自己的期望和信念,从而影响读者的评价观念。White 的新闻结构模型由五部分组成,但这五个部分并不是独自分开,各成一体的,也不是按照紧接之前内容或紧接之后内容的顺序依次展开的,而是以一个环形轨道的模式展开的。在这个模式中,新闻的开篇部分是新闻的核心部分,新闻中的详述、评论、解释、背景四个部分都是围绕着开篇部分详细展开,每一部分论述都与开篇部分遥相呼应,紧密关联,它们组成了一个环形轨道模式。在新闻语篇中,这种结构模型使得新闻内容的联系更加紧密,更具有逻辑性。

评价理论是本书的主要理论框架。本书从介入和态度系统视角分析"一带一路"对外英文新闻语篇,从 White 的环绕

轨道模型新闻结构的五部分来研究"一带一路"对外新闻介入
和态度资源的分布规律,揭示此类语篇的话语策略、韵律模
式、修辞功能和人际意义。

第四章 "一带一路"对外新闻
介入策略定量分析

根据 White(1998)的新闻结构模型,新闻语篇按语义关系分为五部分:开篇、详述、解释、背景、评论。我们先按语类结构对"一带一路"对外新闻的五部分介入策略进行定量分析,总结出"一带一路"对外新闻语篇介入资源的分布规律。

一、介入资源的分布规律

本书根据语类结构的特征对"一带一路"对外新闻的五部分介入策略进行了定量分析,统计出了"一带一路"对外新闻语篇介入资源分布数据(表 4-1),以及介入资源在语篇中的分布趋势(图 4-1)。

通过定量分析,我们发现,新闻报道中涌现出大量的多声话语资源。整体而言,开篇部分和背景部分运用单声策略比较多,解释部分与评论部分运用对话收缩比较多,详述部分运用对话扩展比较多,而在整体布局中,同意、宣布、接纳等介入策略应用比较少,这与新闻语篇各阶段的交际目的密切相关。

表 4-1 "一带一路"对外新闻介入资源分布

介入资源		新闻语篇									
		开篇部分		详述部分		解释部分		评论部分		背景部分	
		数量	比例/%	数量	比例/%	数量	比例/%	数量	比例/%	数量	比例/%
单声		195	45.14	150	23.11	24	9.96	0	0.00	328	66.94
对话收缩	否定	8	1.85	22	3.39	25	10.37	22	10.38	37	7.55
	反对	2	0.46	21	3.23	33	13.69	33	15.57	40	8.16
	同意	0	0.00	0	0.00	9	3.73	12	5.66	0	0.00
	宣布	0	0.00	0	0.00	10	4.15	9	4.24	0	0.00
	支持	53	12.27	43	6.63	117	48.55	105	49.53	52	10.61
	合计	63	14.58	86	13.25	194	80.50	181	85.38	129	26.33
对话扩展	接纳	0	0.00	0	0.00	0	0.00	0	0.00	0	0.00
	承认	169	39.12	391	60.25	15	6.22	18	8.49	32	6.53
	疏远	5	1.16	22	3.39	8	3.32	13	6.13	1	0.20
	合计	174	40.28	413	63.64	23	9.54	31	14.62	33	6.73
总计		432	100.00	649	100.00	241	100.00	212	100.00	490	100.00

在新闻开篇部分与背景部分,新闻作者主要运用单声策略来陈述新闻事实、相关新闻事件以及新闻历史背景,吸引读者注意,展现新闻背景。在解释部分与评论部分,新闻作者在容纳外在声音的同时对某些话语进行了限制,主要是通过官方权威性的话语让读者信服。在详述部分,新闻作者扩大话语空间,特别是频繁运用承认策略,尽可能多地转述他人话语来对新闻内容进行举例或重述,力图向作者更全面客观地还原新闻事件。经过数据统计,我们还发现新闻语篇的五个部分不是各自分离的,详述、评论、解释、背景这四个部分是围绕开篇

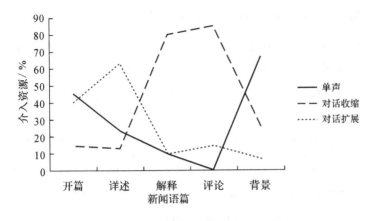

图 4-1　"一带一路"对外新闻介入资源趋势

部分展开,它们组成了一个环形轨道模式,话语空间都是从展开到压缩再到关闭不断循环反复的。上述统计结果体现了我国对外宣传"一带一路"倡议的新闻话语介入策略,有利于我国和沿线国家合作机制的构建和运行。在新闻报道中,作者借助介入资源,在语篇结构中,有策略地彰显"一带一路"倡议内涵和"五通"目标意义,不断调节新闻话语空间,突显新闻语篇立场,赢得新闻读者尊重和认同。

二、开篇部分的介入策略

新闻开篇部分由标题和导语组成,简要介绍新闻的要点,由于这是事实陈述,所以客观性较强,但即使是陈述事实,也能体现新闻语篇的人际意义。上述统计显示,在开篇部分中,运用最显著的策略是单声策略(45.14%)和承认策略(39.12%)。新闻作者运用单声策略不引述任何声音,也不暗示其他观点,话语空间里只有新闻作者的声音,表述的命题是绝对正确的,无须讨论或辩驳的,作者为所述的命题负责。

例如:Chinese President Xi Jinping and his Russian counterpart Vladimir Putin on Wednesday sent congratulatory messages to the opening ceremony of China-Russia local cooperation and exchange.

这是关于中俄地方合作交流年开幕式的一则新闻的导语,在这则导语中,新闻作者仅仅向大家阐述一个事实,而没有引用其他任何声音,如果将其看作对话形式,也就是说作者只提供自己一种立场,没有公开承认其他立场的存在,这样做使大家轻而易举地接受这个事实,也向大家展现了"一带一路"倡议促进了中俄地方合作与交流,推动了共同发展。

在新闻开篇部分中,承认也是一种常见的形式(… said a report released here on Thursday; French President Emmanuel Macron said … ; According to a survey released Friday, …等),新闻作者运用承认策略,转述新闻关键人物的核心话语,提出新闻话题,并且暗示这只是一方或一人之言,使人想到还有其他观点,从而扩展对话空间。

例如：The Belt and Road Initiative offers opportunities in logistics and stimulates supply in China and Britain, a British expert told Xinhua, ahead of an upcoming visit by British Prime Minister Theresa May to Beijing.

这是关于在英国首相特蕾莎·梅访华之前，各界人士热议"一带一路"倡议下，中英双方合作带来的机遇的新闻报道。在新闻的开篇部分中，新闻作者将一位英国专家作为转述对象，彰显其权威性。从引述的话语中可以察觉到英国对于中国"一带一路"倡议的积极响应和高度赞誉，加快了双方贸易协作的步伐。语篇运用承认策略，预留了一定的话语空间，向读者展示中英两国的友好合作发展前景，语篇作者将话语重任放置在英国专家身上，巧妙地规避了责任，并从对方的角度出发，使得话语更有说服力。

由此可见，新闻作者在开篇部分借助单声策略，阐述新闻事实，向读者表达自己的立场和观点，然后通过承认策略，引用别人话语，支持自己观点，邀请多种声音进入对话空间，这样显得转述内容更加客观，呈现给读者中立客观的态度和包容开放的姿态。

三、详述部分的介入策略

新闻详述部分主要是对开篇要素的具体描述，包括举例和重述两个部分内容,重述是必要成分,是对开篇中的新闻元素进行扩展补充,往往紧跟着开篇。然后通过举例来扩展开篇要素,使得详述语步更具体,更生动。上述统计显示,详述部分最主要的介入策略是承认策略(60.25%)和单声策略(23.11%),这与详述部分的交际目的是密切相关的。因为详述部分主要是对新闻事件的具体描述、举例或重述,它要求讲述内容客观真实,使读者能准确了解新闻事件的来龙去脉,让读者信服。新闻作者在详述部分延续了开篇部分的交际目的和介入策略,并且主要以承认策略为主,通过转述他人的话语来表达观点,扩大对话空间,提高了新闻可信度。丰富的转述话语不仅表明新闻语篇信息量大,报道面广,对话空间包容性强,而且在潜移默化中强化了新闻作者观点的普遍性和代表性。新闻作者的转述对象主要有五类:专家学者、政府官员、普通民众、社会企业和媒体记者。这五类转述对象分别涵盖了不同的社会角色,使得新闻报道更加全面。其中使用频率比较高的是政府官员和专家学者,因为"一带一路"倡议属于国家倡议,由政府官员发布和解释"一带一路"相关政策,再由专家学者从各个角度进行补充,有利于增强转述话语的权威性和可信度,提高新闻语篇的说服力,促进读者接受渗透在语篇中的作者观点。

例 1. <u>Experts here said</u> Bangladesh and China have, in the year past, enjoyed very strong relations. <u>They said</u> both countries share many similarities and as such should maintain the momentum of cooperation. (专家学者)

例 2. In "the new era", <u>Xi said</u>, the relations between the two countries could have greater potential, with development under the Belt and Road Initiative and the ambition of jointly building a community of a shared future for mankind. (政府官员)

例 3. China's image is steadily improving, with international appreciation of its performance in domestic and foreign affairs, economic influence and cultural and high-tech hallmarks, <u>according to a survey</u> released Friday. (普通民众)

例 4. <u>Liu Zhaohui, the Assistance Project Manager from China Harbor Engineering Company Ltd.</u> said, "We had finished all the civil engineering of the project by Nov. 2015 …"(社团企业)

例 5. China Development Bank (CDB) will make available up to 10 billion yuan in the next five years to Standard Chartered to facilitate Belt and Road projects, <u>according to a British press release</u>. (媒体记者)

例 1 这则新闻是中国和孟加拉国 2017 年在互利共赢基础上进一步加强友好合作关系。新闻作者采用介入资源的承认策略,转述专家的话语向读者展示了中孟两国在过去就有很深厚的伙伴关系,在"一带一路"倡议下,两国在各个方面有许多相似点,这些相似点促成了中孟两国的进一步合作。在这里新闻作者转述专家的话语,从专业的角度来解析中孟两国的合作关系,增强了语篇的说服力。

例2这则新闻是中国国家主席习近平夫妇在北京会见法国总统马克龙夫妇,习主席强调,在"一带一路"倡议下,中法两国的关系更加深入,为建立人类命运共同体而合作,马克龙也强调将积极参与"一带一路"建设。在这里新闻作者转述政府官员的话语强调了"一带一路"倡议对中法两国的影响,使得新闻更有权威性和说服力。

例3这则新闻是关于一个全球的民意调查,调查结果显示:在"一带一路"倡议下,中国的国际形象不断改善,经济、文化、科技等在国际上的影响力也有了巨大飞跃,"一带一路"倡议获得了越来越多国家的认可。在这里新闻作者运用介入资源的承认策略,以普通民众的调查结果向读者展示"一带一路"倡议给中国带来的巨大影响,具有强烈的感染力。

例4这则新闻的主要内容是在2017年,在斯里兰卡的汉班托塔地区,中国和斯里兰卡建立了合资企业,从而使得两国进一步合作的愿景变成了现实。中国港口工程有限公司的项目经理助理刘朝晖表示已经完成了此项目的所有国内工程,并在今年内全部发放到汉班托塔的项目地区。新闻作者转述刘朝晖的话语向广大读者展现了"一带一路"倡议下中国和斯里兰卡的合作成为现实,提高了"一带一路"倡议在当地的影响力。

例 5 这则新闻的主要内容是中英两国共同在"一带一路"项目建设上的投资合作。英国媒体表示,中国发展银行在未来五年内将向渣打银行投入 100 亿元作为"一带一路"项目建设的投资。这数据充分表明中英两国在"一带一路"项目建设上的合作投入是巨大的,以英国新闻媒体的视角展现数字结果充分表明事件的可靠性。

综上所述,新闻作者在详述部分充分运用承认策略,转述不同对象的话语,丰富转述内容,旨在增强转述内容的权威性和可信度,提高新闻语篇的说服力,促进读者接受渗透在语篇里的作者的观点。

四、解释部分的介入策略

新闻解释部分包括原因和结果两个部分,旨在表明新闻要素的前因后果,新闻事件发生的缘由和影响,增强新闻报道的逻辑性,便于读者更深入地了解新闻的来龙去脉。如表4-1显示,在解释部分中,新闻作者主要使用介入策略的对话收缩策略。主要表现为支持策略(48.55%)和反对策略(13.69%)。常见的支持策略形式为"the trade minister confirmed that…, the ambassador pointed out that…等",新闻作者通过该策略来支持被引述内容的合理性和可靠性,主动承担被引述内容的相关责任,促使读者认同被转述内容的观点,这与解释部分的交际目的也是密不可分的。解释部分主要解释新闻事件的原因和结果,新闻作者运用支持策略,支持被引述的观点,使得内外声音具有一致性,这种收缩模式突显了被引述的声音,压制其他反对声音,从而缩小话语空间。

例如:For foreign firms, it increasingly pays to use Chinese yuan, Cao pointed out. Using the yuan in trade and investment will make it easier and cheaper for foreign firms to do business with China, while including the yuan into investment portfolios will help optimize investment structure and return.

这则新闻是报道中国进一步打开国际市场,促进国际贸易和投资,中国人民币在国际市场上发挥着越来越重要的作用。中银国际研究院的主席曹远征指出,人民币在中外贸易中也发挥着越来越重要的作用,人民币不仅可以使外国公司的贸易和投资更加便捷,而且使用人民币还可以优化投资结构和回报。新闻作者在这里运用介入资源的支持策略,明确认同曹远征的观点,向读者解释了人民币在全球贸易中发挥重大作用的原因:自从"一带一路"倡议实施以来,中国始终以"五通"发展为目标,"五通"在"一带一路"建设中发挥着重要的作用,中国的国际地位迅速上升,在对外贸易和投资过程中,人民币也日益发挥着重要的作用。

反对策略是说话人用某一观点去取代已有的立场和观点,常见于一些用于引导转折关系或让步关系的连接词中。在"一带一路"对外新闻中,新闻作者运用了大量的转折词汇(Nevertheless, China is still committed to …;The project was suspended,but the minister said…等),以此来用一种观点取代或反对另外一种可能在此出现的观点,从而与读者建立了一种一致的关系,形成评价同盟。

Although China and the members of Community of Latin American and Caribbean States are geographically far apart,they are all developing nations and they share a common aspiration for peace, prosperity and people's happiness,Xi said.

这则新闻主要内容是在"一带一路"倡议的号召下,中国加深了与拉美共同体国家间的合作。拉美共同体是西半球最大的区域性政治组织,拉美共同体成为拉美对外对话合作的代表。习主席在访问巴西期间,会见了拉美共同体的领导人,为建立中国与拉丁美洲和加勒比地区关系的区域性论坛做了前期准备,才得以使区域性论坛顺利召开,双方合作关系进一步加强。在上述例子中,新闻作者转述习主席的话语,指出虽然中国与拉共体成员之间的地理位置相距甚远,但是他们和中国都是发展中国家,都有着促进经济繁荣、世界和平和人民幸福的共同愿望,他们的合作是不受地域限制,是大势所趋。在这里,新闻作者把一种期待——地域相隔太远的国家不会进行合作——投射到读者身上,跟读者建立了一致的联系。但是跟通常的期待相反,作者运用"Although"这个转折词汇,表示尽管地域相隔太远,但彼此有着共同愿望,也可以进行紧密合作。作者运用反对策略,反对了另一个可能在此出现的观点,即由于地理位置相距遥远,中国和拉美国家在各方面都有很大区别。由此表明"一带一路"倡议是一个开放包容、互利共赢的政策,是符合实现双方共同愿望的政策,中国与拉共体的合作是"一带一路"倡议实施的一个结晶。

可见,新闻作者在解释部分通过支持策略来转述他人话语,佐证自己观点,同时利用反对策略来暗示并反驳相反立场,增强作者说理和阐释的逻辑性,这充分体现了介入策略的人际意义和解释部分的交际目的。

五、评论部分的介入策略

新闻评论部分是对开篇部分中新闻事件的社会意义、情感影响等进行点评,评论的对象既可以是新闻事件,也可以是新闻人物,目的是表明新闻事件的社会影响和新闻人物的价值取向。如表 4-1 所示,新闻作者评论部分主要运用支持策略(49.53%)和反对策略(15.57%),支持策略引述的内容都是对"一带一路"政策的肯定和认可,反对策略往往是澄清误解,通过对比突显"一带一路"倡议的优越性。

例如:Alicia Barcena, the United Nation executive secretary of the Economic Commission for Latin American and the Caribbean, points out that China can provide the Latin American region with more opportunities under the frame of the Belt and Road Initiative.

这则新闻主要内容是在"一带一路"倡议下,中国对拉美和加勒比经济地区的投资对促进当地经济增长和提高人们生活水平带来了积极影响。新闻作者运用支持策略,转述联合国拉丁美洲和加勒比经济委员会执行秘书艾丽西亚·巴塞纳的话语,指出在"一带一路"倡议下,中国为拉美地区提供了更多的发展机会。这是对"一带一路"倡议的肯定和认可,新闻作者赞同转述话语,主动与转述对象结成评价同盟,无形中压制或排斥了其他不同立场,收缩了对话空间。这表明,新闻作者认为转述对象具有足够的权威性,足以赢得大部分读者的认同,因此通过支持策略表明态度,巩固与读者的同盟关系。

例如:Despite the shrinking value, the quality of M&As (mergers and acquisitions) by Chinese companies improved, Guo said. The report showed areas including technology, industry and consumption were favored by Chinese investors.

　　这则新闻的主要内容是在"一带一路"沿线地区,中国企业数量迅速增长,但由于国家对外投资的监管力度加强,被中国公司并购的企业价值相比 2017 年有所降低,但中国公司的并购质量有所改善。新闻作者在此运用反对策略向读者表明另一种潜在观点,即企业价值的降低意味着中国企业并购质量随之降低,然后果断推翻这一观点,并明确提出相反观点,即企业价值的降低并不代表"一带一路"政策的弊端,而是提高了并购质量,使得企业在"一带一路"政策的引导下不断改进,从而不仅向读者表明作者考虑全面,为读者而想,而且消除了读者误解,达到了赢得读者信任、说服读者的交际目的。

　　可见,新闻作者在评论部分运用支持策略引述的内容是对"一带一路"政策的认可和肯定,运用反对策略往往是澄清误解,通过对比突出"一带一路"政策的优越性。两种介入策略的交替使用显示了新闻语篇的评价立场,也彰显了"一带一路"政策的重要意义。

六、背景部分的介入策略

　　新闻背景部分是为开篇部分中新闻要素提供背景材料,包括对比类似事件、回顾事件背景等,在新闻背景部分,新闻作者可通过描述类似事件,引导读者以此为参照对新闻事件进行价值判断,作者也可通过回顾事件背景,呈现事件的来龙去脉,引导读者深度解读新闻语篇。如表 4-1 所示,新闻作者在背景部分主要运用介入策略中的单声策略(66.94%)和支持策略(10.61%)。单声策略主要是提供新闻的背景材料,描述新闻事件的发展过程,支持策略主要转述新闻当事人或专家学者的话语,通过他人话语来描述类似事件,引导读者进行新闻事件对比,影响读者的阅读立场和评价姿态。

例如:Chinese yuan's globalization journey generally started from piloting RMB settlement in cross-border trade in 2009 and picked up pace in 2016 when the IMF included the yuan in the basket of currencies that make up the Special Drawing Right, an alternative reserve asset to the dollar.

这则新闻的主要内容是中国人民币在全球经济贸易中的影响力,新闻作者运用单声策略向读者展示中国人民币全球化进程的背景,在"一带一路"建设中,中国的国际地位逐渐上升,与世界各国的贸易日益频繁,与此同时人民币的作用日益凸显,可以作为另一种储备资产在国际社会中发挥它独特的作用。在这里新闻作者只提供了一种立场,向读者表明人民币全球化这个事件的历史背景以及发展进程,从而使读者更清楚地了解人民币全球化的相关内容。新闻作者认为,该背景信息是历史事实，无须与读者协商立场，作者愿意为此内容承担全部责任。

例如：Chinese President Xi Jinping has <u>pointed out</u> that China sees the 16 + 1 cooperation between China and 16 central and eastern European countries as an important gateway to incorporate the Belt and Road Initiative into the European economic circle.

这则新闻主要阐述在"一带一路"倡议下，中国与中东欧的 16 个国家进行合作，并被纳入欧洲经济圈。新闻作者运用支持策略，转述习主席的观点，认为中国与中东欧 16 个国家的合作是"一带一路"倡议所带来的积极影响。作为"一带一路"倡议的其中一项成果，类似于这样的合作不胜枚举。作者明确支持此观点，目的是表达在"一带一路"倡议下，中国与沿线国家乃至世界各国的合作都呈现出良好发展势头。

综上所述，作者在新闻的背景部分运用单声策略和支持策略是符合新闻背景的交际目的的。为了宣传"一带一路"政策的效果和影响，新闻作者在回顾新闻事件背景时，运用单声策略构建封闭的话语空间，向读者表明事件的描述是真实的、无可争议的。在描述类似的新闻事件时，运用支持策略转述新闻当事人或专家学者的话语，既体现新闻报道的客观性和真实性，又表明新闻作者的立场，收缩语篇对话空间，巩固与读者的评价联盟。

七、介入策略的韵律话语模式

上述对"一带一路"对外新闻各部分介入策略的分析显示,开篇和详述部分介入策略相同,都以单声策略和承认策略为主,话语空间从关闭到打开并不断扩展;解释和评论部分介入策略类似,通过支持和反对策略,不断收缩对话空间;背景部分以支持策略和单声策略为主,话语空间不断收缩直至关闭。我们发现,"一带一路"对外新闻的介入策略随着各阶段交际目的的变化表现出韵律性话语模式。开篇部分中,新闻作者为了引起读者兴趣,力求言简意赅,往往以单声策略呈现新闻标题,同时为了展现客观中立的报道风格,用承认策略推出新闻导语,以开放姿态包容各种声音和立场,话语空间由此打开。详述部分是对话空间最开放的阶段,新闻作者为了尽可能真实还原新闻事件,充分利用承认策略,转述新闻参与者话语,为读者创造亲临新闻现场之感。解释部分通过缜密阐释,为读者揭开新闻事件各元素间的逻辑关系,消除读者心中潜在的迷惑,排除一些杂音并缩小对话空间。评论部分力图聚焦观点,压缩话语空间,影响读者对新闻事件的价值判断和评价立场,拉拢读者结成同盟。背景部分往往通过单声描述类似事件,在封闭话语空间里,用公认的事实来对比眼前的新闻,引导读者接受新闻作者的评价立场。由此可见,"一带一路"对外新闻各阶段的交际目的决定了介入策略和评价姿态：从吸引读者眼球、为读者罗列事实，到解读来龙去脉、影响读者立场，以及点评新闻事件、与读者建立同盟，介入策略随之表现出韵律般模式，对话空间时而扩展，时而收缩，声音此起彼伏，交相辉映。

通过对"一带一路"对外新闻各部分介入策略的分析显示，随着此类新闻语篇的展开，话语空间呈现"关闭——扩展——收缩——关闭"的趋势，表现出韵律般模式，充分体现了语篇不同阶段的交际目的和评价立场。

第五章 "一带一路"对外新闻
介入策略定性分析

语域理论是系统功能语言学的重要理论。以 Halliday 为代表的系统功能学派特别强调语境的作用，他们认为语言在一定语境中发生，并在一定语境中被理解或得到解释，也可以说语言特征是受语境支配的。Halliday(1978)把决定语言特征的语境因素归纳为三种：语场、语旨、语式。"语场"是指实际发生的事，或者是语言发生的环境，包括谈论的话题；"语旨"是指参与者之间的关系，包括参与者的社会地位，以及他们之间的角色关系；"语式"是指语言交际的渠道或媒介，比如是口头的还是书面的，是即兴的还是有准备的。语境三要素中任何一项的改变都会引起话语意义的变化，从而引起语言的变异，产生不同的语域。人们一旦在学习中掌握了语域理论的基本规律，就能根据语境预测语篇，也能根据语篇预测发生的情境。这种双向预测性在新闻语篇分析中有很大实用价值。

"一带一路"是中国与丝路沿途国家分享优质产能、共商项目投资、共建基础设施、共享合作成果的倡议，内容包括政策沟通、设施联通、贸易畅通、资金融通、民心相通等"五通"目标,因为"五通"发展各有侧重,国家在"五通"发展方面会采取不同举措,新闻作者也会根据不同交际目的而采取相应话语介入策略。下面将从中国一带一路网上的"五通"发展角度各选一篇新闻报道进行具体分析,阐明"一带一路"倡议下"五通"发展对外新闻的语域特征和语类结构中各阶段交际目的如何影响语篇介入策略的韵律话语模式。

一、"政策沟通"语篇的介入策略

"政策沟通"是"一带一路"建设中的政府行为,也是沿线各国实现互利共赢的政策法律保障,是"五通"发展中的关键环节,地位突出,作用重要,举足轻重(孙力,2016)。加强政策沟通,各国可以就经济发展战略和对策进行充分交流,本着求同存异原则,协商制订推进区域合作的规划和措施,在政策和法律上为区域经济融合"开绿灯"。目前,在"一带一路"倡议沟通方面,中国和沿线国家都进行了有益探索,并取得了较好成效。

在"一带一路"倡议实施过程中,中国与沿线国家在经济、政治、文化等方面制定了相应政策,例如,习近平主席与巴西前总统特梅尔积极探讨"一带一路"投资伙伴计划对接;中国与巴勒斯坦完成自贸协定联合可行性研究;习近平主席同南非总统会谈,加强在"一带一路"中非合作论坛框架内合作;王毅同利比亚团结政府外长会谈签署共建"一带一路"谅解备忘录等。这些政策促进了中国和沿线国家的共同发展。下面以2017年7月11日发表在中国一带一路网上题为"G20 consensus highlights cooperation as major trend in global governance"的新闻为例,阐明介入策略在"政策沟通"新闻语篇中的运用模式和人际意义,以及在此类语篇结构中的韵律话语模式。新闻原文如下:

G20 consensus highlights cooperation as major trend in global governance

Chinese President Xi Jinping and other leaders attending the 12th Summit of the Group of 20（G20）major economies pose for a group photo in Hamburg, Germany, July 7, 2017.

The consensus reached at the just-concluded Group of 20（G20）major economies on support for globalization highlights multilateral cooperation as a major trend in global governance that meets people's needs.

Meanwhile, experts said China is playing an increasingly important role in global governance, bringing up new ideas and initiatives.

Leaders at the G20 summit themed "Shaping an Interconnected World" held on July 7-8 in the German city of Hamburg pledged support for continued globalization with a call for opening markets and opposing protectionism. They also agreed to work towards a stable international trading system and more cross-border investments.

The G20 summit consensus conforms to the new circumstances of the global economy, which is now marked by both interdependence and instability, according to experts.

Dennis J. Snower, co-chairman of Think 20, a think tank for the G20, believes such a global economy calls for multilateral solutions.

The global economy is "basically and completely integrated," so the problems generated are also interdependent, such as climate change, the financial crisis, cyber security and terrorism, he said.

"These problems cross national boundaries and can only be solved multilaterally," said Snower, who is also president of the Kiel Institute for the World Economy.

Dirk Messner, co-chairman of Think 20, noticed the dramatic changes over the last three years are posing new challenges to the G20 group.

Messner, also director of the German Development Institute, cited Britain's exit from the European Union and

U. S. President Donald Trump's protectionist "America First" policies and withdrawal from the Paris Climate Agreement as being among the major events to put globalization and multilateralism at risk.

He said the year 2016 was "a shock" and "very difficult for multilateralism" due to Trump, after the Paris climate deal was reached and the United Nations (UN) Sustainable Development Agenda for 2030 signed in 2015.

However, the political and economic instabilities indicate the changing needs of the people, he added.

Global governance "should above all answer to men's needs," which go beyond material prosperity to social ones such as the need for life satisfaction and security, he noted.

Messner believes that as a premier forum on international cooperation and global governance, the G20 group should address more major concerns of people in global development, such as climate change and the widening gap between rich and poor, helping shape a peaceful and hopeful future for the world.

Regarding global governance to meet the new changes, the importance of China is increasing in many aspects, Messner said.

China was regarded as a powerful spokesman for global

multilateralism at the Hamburg summit, said Shada Islam, policy director of Friends of Europe, a leading Brussels-based think tank.

At the summit, Chinese President Xi Jinping delivered an important speech with proposals made urging efforts to continue opening-up and inclusiveness as well as to push for interconnectivity and growth.

Shi Shiwei, professor with the Free University of Berlin, said, "Xi's speech represents the stance of developing countries," and "shows China is a firm advocate for globalization and multilateralism, and it is braving more responsibilities in global governance."

Xi's speech, Shi said, stresses implementation of the UN 2030 agenda, insistence on sustainable and inclusive growth, integration of economic and social policies and support for further globalization while containing its ills.

Snower deems Xi's proposals on G20 cooperation in the digital economy and new industrial revolution as being "of great importance," which requires the joint action of developed and developing countries under the multilateral framework.

Thomas Heberer, a well-known China watcher from Duisburg-Essen University, said Xi has assumed "the major role" of promoting a cooperative and open world economy.

Helga Zepp-LaRouche, chief of the Schiller Institute think tank in Germany, said Xi's speech made it clear that the China-proposed Belt and Road Initiative is "highly compatible" with the G20 goal, and was making the initiative's core values such as win-win cooperation and a community of shared destiny for mankind into new principles of global governance. "This is working," she said.

The Belt and Road Initiative aims to build infrastructure and trade networks connecting Asia with Africa and Europe along the ancient Silk Road trade routes in order to seek common development and prosperity. The initiative, being the embodiment of China's proposals, carries cooperation plans for infrastructure construction, unimpeded trade and capital flows, among others. This shows that as an economic power, China is shouldering its leadership role.

该新闻的语场是在2017年德国汉堡举行的第12届G20峰会上达成的G20共识,强调加强多边合作,促进全球治理。该语场肯定了"一带一路"倡议所倡导的合作共赢的重要性。语旨是新闻机构和读者,新闻机构是中国一带一路网,它是专门对外报道"一带一路"的官方新闻网站,读者是想了解"一带一路"政策的外国人士。语式是以文字形式通过网络呈现的书面语。该新闻语篇结构各部分依次展开顺序如下:开篇——详述——解释——评论——详述——解释——评论——背景。

在开篇部分,新闻作者运用单声策略向读者陈述了德国汉堡第 12 届 G20 峰会这个事件,点明新闻的语场是"The consensus reached at the just-concluded Group of 20(G20) major economies on support for globalization highlights multilateral cooperation as a major trend in global governance that meets people's needs"。在这里,新闻作者运用单声策略,向读者呈现一个不容置疑的事实,即 G20 达成共识,意在加强多边合作,最终目的是以满足人们需求为出发点,促进世界各国的共同治理。新闻作者运用单声策略,关闭对话空间,表明开篇内容即 G20 达成的共识是毋庸置疑的,从而压制了新闻读者的其他想法与猜测,促使读者接受 G20 共识的价值判断。除了单声策略,新闻作者在开篇部分还运用了承认策略(Meanwhile, experts said China is playing an increasingly important role in global governance …)。此处,作者转述专家们的话语,表明中国在全球治理上发挥了日益重要的作用。新闻作者运用承认策略,转述外部话语和观点,不仅扩大了对话空间,也表明自己中立的态度,让读者相信并不是作者自己在宣扬"一带一路",而是专家们的结论,从而赢得读者信任,引导读者接受语篇立场,即中国"一带一路"倡议在全球治理中发挥重大作用,为实现全球共同治理提出了中国方案。

在详述部分(Leaders at the G20 summit themed "Shaping an Interconnected World" …),新闻作者首先运用单声策略陈述了德国汉堡 G20 峰会的具体内容。峰会的主题是"塑造互联世界",呼吁开放市场,反对保护主义,希望建立一个稳定的国际贸易体系。紧接着作者运用承认策略(… according to experts; Dennis J. Snower believes …),转述专家以及 G20 智囊团联合主席 Dennis J. Snower 的话语,表明 G20 峰会共识适用于当今全球经济相互依赖和复杂多变的新环境,而全球经济的发展是需要国际合作的。作者没有直接阐述这个观点,而是引用权威人士的话语向读者表明多国合作是新时代的需要,是大势所趋。由此作者打开了对话空间,容纳不同的话语声音,表现出新闻报道不是一家之言,更能体现新闻语篇的客观性,也体现了多国合作的必要性。

在解释部分,新闻作者通过支持策略(… he noted … ; Messner cited …)来说明为什么全球治理要加强国际合作。我们处于一个经济全球化和世界多极化的社会,因此各国的经济、政治、文化等是相互影响的,与此同时,各国面临的问题比如全球变暖、金融危机、网络安全和恐怖主义等也是普遍存在、相互交织的。这些全球共同面对的问题仅仅靠个人或单一国家的力量是无法解决的,所以只有多国合作,才能合力解决这些全球问题。在此,新闻作者为了强调国际合作与全球治理的因果关系,运用支持策略,明确支持来自专家学者和权威人士的外部观点,缩小了对话空间,亲自为引用的话语负责。新闻作者相信引述对象的权威性和话语内容可以说服读者,也与作者自己立场一致,因此通过支持策略表明自己与引述对象已经结成评价同盟,引导读者接受该评价立场。除此之外,作者运用反对策略(… however …)来说明一切政策的制定都要以人民利益为出发点。目前世界政治经济的发展都存在不稳定性,但作者运用"however"这个转折词,反对了另一个可能在此出现的观点:随着巴黎气候协定和联合国可持续发展协议的签署,各国的担忧得以缓解,世界政治经济局势应该趋于稳定。作者运用反对策略将一种信念投射到读者身上,那就是目前的政治、经济局势的转变是由人们利益变化决定的,是根据人们需求的转变而变化的,充分体现了为读者所想,以及缜密逻辑和全面思考,促使读者与作者形成评价同盟,接受语篇的立场:G20 共识(即国际合作和全球治理)旨在维护全人类根本利益,着眼于人类未来发展,致力于各国共同繁荣。

在评论部分,新闻作者继续运用支持策略(shows …; deems …; made it clear that …)来阐明中国支持全球化和多边主义,中国提出的"一带一路"倡议与 G20 共识的目标是一致的。在这里,新闻作者进一步压缩对话空间,突显语篇立场,巩固与读者的评价联盟,强调中国"一带一路"倡议致力于合作互赢,打造"人类命运共同体"。作者通过运用支持策略引述外部声音,力图说服读者接受作者的评价立场,认同"一带一路"倡议对全球治理的贡献。

紧接着新闻作者详述了习主席在 G20 峰会上的报告、提出的政策以及相关影响,并解释了"一带一路"倡议与全球治理的关系,转述别人的观点来评论中国在全球治理方面取得的重大成就,话语空间也因此再次扩展与收缩。

在最后的背景部分,新闻作者运用单声策略描述新闻事件的背景,习主席参加了德国汉堡的 G20 峰会,在会上阐述了"一带一路"倡议旨在加强与古代丝绸之路沿线国家在基础设施、资金、贸易等方面的合作,促进彼此间共同发展和繁荣。在这里作者运用单声策略,关闭了对话空间,目的是向读者展示"一带一路"倡议的目标和实践成果是有目共睹、无可争议的,"一带一路"倡议符合 G20 共识的目标,符合全球治理的发展趋势,从而获得读者认可。

由此可见,该语篇的介入策略就是通过介入资源调控新闻语篇话语空间,随着语篇展开,各阶段交际目的变化,话语空间时而扩展,时而收缩,不断与读者进行态度磋商,试图说服读者接受语篇立场,建立评价联盟,认可中国在政策沟通方面所做的努力和取得的成果,支持中国对外政策沟通的立场和见解:"一带一路"倡议下的政策沟通,内涵深刻,外延广阔,致力于提升中国和沿线国家间政治互信,形成合作意向,对接战略规划和发展蓝图,向合作国家宣传中国提倡的全新合作模式和理念,争取沿线国家的积极响应和参与,实现"共商,共建,共享"。"共商"就是通过沟通,倡导"和平合作,包容开放,求同存异,互利共赢"的丝路精神,探求符合沿线各国和人民根本利益的全新合作模式。

政策沟通的目的就是让沿线国家对"一带一路"建设原则、内涵和途径等关键议题达成共识,建构沿线国家间多层次、多维度政府间经济发展规划、宏观经济战略、重大合作项目对接的工作机制,实现基本趋同、利益共享的决策、政策、计划和规则,从而构建坚强的"责任共同体""利益共同体"和"命运共同体"。作为新兴经济体的代表,中国奉行全球化宗旨,并为全球化而努力。正如语篇所示,"The Consensus reached at the just-concluded Group of 20 (G20) major economies on support for globalization highlights multilateral cooperation as a major trend in global governance that meets people's needs"。世界主要经济体已经达成共识,全球化和多边合作是治理世界的大势所趋,也是各国人民的需求所在。通过单声资源,语篇把各国关于全球化的立场构建成毋庸置疑的客观事实,随后借助介入资源中的承认策略,引述专家学者话语,表现中国为全球化所做的努力(Experts said China is playing an increasingly important role in global governance, bringing up new ideas and initiatives)。通过扩展话语空间,营造开放包容、客观公正的评价基调,旨在赢得读者信任,引导读者接受语篇观点。

习近平主席在此次 G20 峰会上发表重要演讲,提出倡议,敦促各国齐心协力,继续开放市场,深化融合,推动互联发展(Chinese President Xi Jinping delivered an important speech with proposals made urging efforts to continue opening-up and inclusiveness as well as to push for interconnectivity and growth)。通过单声策略,语篇把习主席的演讲要点构建成客观事实,无须与读者磋商,随后利用各种多声策略,引述国外专家话语,高度赞扬习主席的讲话(Shi Shiwei, professor with the Free University of Berlin, said …; Snower deems Xi's proposal …; Thomas Heberer, a well-known China watcher from Duisburg-Essen University, said …)。此种介入策略在该语篇中经常出现:首先利用单声资源构建封闭的话语空间,用陈述事实的方式呈现观点,然后通过多声资源打开话语空间,用转述话语的形式支持观点,营造和谐统一、客观公正、包容开放的评价立场,潜移默化中影响读者阅读立场,和读者结成评价联盟。其实,2017 年习主席在出席瑞士达沃斯世界经济论坛并发表演说时,也表达了类似的观点:困扰世界的很多问题,并不是经济全球化造成的。历史地看,经济全球化是社会生产力发展的客观要求和科技进步的必然结果。经济全球化为世界经济增长提供了强劲动力,促进了商品和资本流动、科技和文明进步、各国人民交往。可见,习主席在多个国际场合,向世界阐释"一带一路"的宗旨,以及中国对全球化和多边主义的一贯立场。

　　目前世界发展日新月异,变化复杂深刻,全球经济情况变化多端,各国都需要应对复杂严峻的发展挑战。语篇运用承认策略,通过转述专家话语,表现目前全球经济新局面(The G20 summit consensus conforms to the new circumstances of the global economy, which is now marked by both interdependence and instability, according to experts)。想要在新一轮经济复苏中取得发展,就需要探索全新合作模式、合作理念与合作平台。正如语篇报道,"The global economy is 'basically and completely integrated,' so the problems generated are also interdependent, such as climate change, the financial crisis, cyber security and terrorism, he said. 'These problems cross national boundaries and can only be solved multilaterally,' said Snower"。此处,通过转述Snower话语,表明全球经济面临的种种问题是全世界、全人类的共同问题,因此解决方案也必须超越国界,需要全球协同合作。"一带一路"倡议正是顺应了当今时代要求,从2013年提出至今,获得了沿线国家的普遍认可,各国政府表现出积极参与的愿望。但是,面对当前纷繁复杂的世界经济和政治局势,许多沿线国家不清楚如何全面融入"一带一路"建设,因此,深入广泛地进行政策沟通,对于顺利推进"一带一路"倡议至关重要,主要涉及政治互信、国际主张、政策制定、合作共识等。

　　首先,政治互信是维护中国和沿线国家社会稳定和谐的基本条件。"China was regarded as a powerful spokesman for global multilateralism at the Hamburg summit，said Shada Islam，policy director of Friends of Europe，a leading Brussels-based think tank"，如语篇所示，中国已经被视为全球多边主义的代言人，而全球化和多边主义作为世界发展的趋势已经得到大多数国家的认可，这说明中国在国际政治场合已经赢得了信任和支持。

其次，关于重大全球议题，如英国脱欧、贸易保护主义、巴黎气候协定等，中国秉承"命运共同体"的原则和精神，提出国际主张，突显大国风范。语篇引述 Dirk Messner，co-chairman of Think 20 的观点，"Britain's exit from the European Union and U.S. President Donald Trump's protectionist "America First" policies and withdrawal from the Paris Climate Agreement as being among the major events to put globalization and multilateralism at risk"。运用介入资源（cited），突显以上转述观点，表明语篇支持该观点，在开放包容的对话氛围中，缩小话语空间，从而在保持新闻报道客观性的同时，把读者的关注点聚焦在当前世界所面临的挑战：英国脱欧、美国贸易保护主义和退出巴黎气候协定。接着，语篇通过反对策略（However）和支持策略（noted），提出当前全球政治和经济动荡的局势表明了世界人民日益变化的需求，而全球共同治理首先要满足人类共同的需求的观点。此处的话语空间伸缩有序，把语篇立场与引述观点紧密结合,形成稳固的评价联盟,进一步加强转述对象的权威性和语篇的客观性。随后,语篇利用承认策略(said),继续转述 Messner 的观点(Regarding global governance to meet the new changes, the importance of China is increasing in many aspects),结合之前的转述内容,表明中国全方位参与全球治理,致力于应对全世界共同面临的挑战,其重要性与日俱增,体现了"人类命运共同体"的中国主张,展示了中国作为发展中国家的责任担当和宽广胸襟。

再次,中国与沿线各国在政策制定方面,目前集中在宏观框架信息的互通交流。语篇通过承认策略,转述专家话语"Xi's speech, Shi said, stresses implementation of the UN 2030 agenda, insistence on sustainable and inclusive growth, integration of economic and social policies and support for further globalization while containing its ills"。习主席强调实施联合国 2030 议程的重要性,该议程是联合国为世界未来十年制定的发展蓝图,符合世界各国的共同利益,为各国政府制定各自发展规划和政策提供了指导意见。例如:坚持可持续性和包容性发展,经济和社会政策融合,支持深化全球化并遏制其弊端。随后,语篇运用支持策略,突显习主席对多边合作框架的深刻理解(Snower deems Xi's proposals on G20 cooperation in the digital economy and new industrial revolution as being "of great importance", which requires the joint action of developed and developing countries under the multilateral framework)。发达国家和发展中国家之间的多边合作框架对于推动数字经济发展和新产业革命至关重要,准确体现了当前世界经济发展的本质、规律和关键,充分表现习主席的远见卓识和大局观念。

最后,在合作共识方面,中国坚持"共建共享",探索共同治理全球的模式和理论,以符合国际经济新秩序的要求,尤其是合作模式的创新,更注重与沿线各国的取长补短,利益共享,理念趋同,以此获得沿线国家的支持和赞赏。在语篇结尾处,通过单声策略,关闭对话空间,重申"一带一路"倡议的宗旨和原则(The Belt and Road Initiative aims to build infrastructure and trade networks connecting Asia with Africa and Europe along the ancient Silk Road trade routes in order to seek common development and prosperity)。沿着古代丝绸之路,建设基础设施和贸易网络,连接亚洲、非洲和欧洲,寻求共同发展和繁荣,这充分体现了中国倡导的全新合作模式,即世界互联,共同发展,共享繁荣(The initiative, being the embodiment of China's proposals, carries cooperation plans for infrastructure construction, unimpeded trade and capital flows, among others),"一带一路"倡议体现了中国方案的精髓,合作共荣是"五通"发展的关键。整个语篇以单声收尾,明确语篇立场(This shows that as an economic power, China is shouldering its leadership role),突显中国作为"一带一路"倡议的提出者,也是世界经济强国,勇于担当,正在以实际行动,呼吁并带领各国共同应对挑战,齐心协力,推进世界经济复苏,共享合作成果。

自从"一带一路"倡议提出以来,沿线各国从观望到接触、从了解到参与,不断融入"一带一路"建设,这期间中国政府和社会各界对外宣传解读政策起到了关键作用。中国媒体和政府机构向世界阐释"一带一路"倡议的内涵和目标,沿线国家政府、企业和当地百姓需要理解中国对该倡议的宗旨解读和发展规划,中国也希望获取沿线各国对共建"一带一路"的建设性意见,以实现"集思广益、共商共建"。

二、"设施联通"语篇的介入策略

"设施联通"是"一带一路"建设的重要基础和优先合作领域,是促进沿线国家经济发展,造福广大人民,提升地区福祉的重要支撑,是实现务实合作、互利共赢的重要依托。"一带一路"建设以来,我国与"一带一路"沿线国家在能源、交通、通信等基础设施领域进行了广泛合作,促进了各国经济发展。

在实施"一带一路"倡议中,我国帮助沿线国家建设大量基础设施,例如:中国已与"一带一路"沿线 62 个国家签订航空运输协定,中俄推进东西天然气管道项目建设,援马尔代夫中马友谊大桥主桥合拢贯通等。下面以 2017 年 4 月 14 日发表在中国一带一路网上题为"Belt and Road Initiative opens up new prospects for China-Jordan cooperation"的新闻为例,阐明介入资源在"设施联通"新闻语篇中的运用策略和人际意义,以及语类结构中各阶段交际目的如何影响语篇介入策略的韵律话语模式。新闻原文如下:

B&R Initiative opens up new prospects for China-Jordan cooperation

The infrastructure projects by Chinese enterprises bring tangible benefits to local residents in Jordan, an important country along the routes of the Belt and Road Initiative, *People's Daily* reports.

Chinese enterprises, with their capital, equipment and technology, are popular in Jordan, a Jordanian newspaper comments.

A water supply network upgrading project conducted with Chinese aid in Zarqa, Jordan has recently been completed. It took the project undertaker, China Geo-Engineering Corporation (CGC) Middle East Branch, six months (three months in advance of schedule), to build the 3.37-kilometer long water pipeline.

Zhang Shuibao, vice manager of the branch, said, "Our workers overcame many difficulties to complete the project. We are deeply moved by local people visiting us with roast meat and fruits."

The pipeline can deliver 520 cubic meters of water per hour to meet the needs of half a million residents, who previously could only have three to four hours of water supply a week.

After fulfilling the add-on cycle power plant contract of Samra's phase II projects in 2010, China's Shandong Electric Power Construction Corp III Electric Power Construction Corp. (SEPCO III) again became the EPC contractor for Samra's Phase IV add-on combined cycle project and Hussein combined-cycle power plant in 2016.

The newly-signed two projects are also expected to effectively help solve power shortage in Jordan once finished.

Hu Shangxiu, the Hussein project's manager assistant, said, "Winning these bids shows that Jordan has trust in us."

The Hussein project has created more than 1,000 jobs for the locals.

Hu advocates China-Jordan cooperation in areas including energy and infrastructure as a good example for bilateral capacity cooperation. The projects have boosted local economic development via creating job opportunities and project procurements.

Also，Guangdong Yudean Group is cooperating with power companies from Malaysia and Estonia to build Attarat Power Plant，which will become Jordan's largest power plant when it is finished in 2020 and will supply 10 to 15 percent of the country's power consumption. China provided around US $ 1. 6 billion in fund for the US $ 2. 1-billion-worth project.

　　该新闻的语场是在"一带一路"倡议下,中国企业在基础设施建设方面,特别是供水设施和供电设施方面给予了约旦人民实质性的帮助,为两国合作创造了新前景。该语场肯定了"一带一路"倡议对约旦人民的积极影响。语旨是新闻机构和读者,新闻机构是中国一带一路网,它是中国政府对外发布"一带一路"新闻的官方网站,读者是海内外关注"一带一路"建设的各界人士。语式是在网站上以文字形式呈现的新闻语篇。该新闻语篇结构各部分依次展开顺序如下:开篇——详述——解释——评论——背景。

　　在新闻开篇部分,新闻作者运用单声策略撰写新闻标题,即"一带一路"倡议为中国和约旦的合作开辟了新前景。在这里作者直接肯定了"一带一路"倡议对两国发展的影响力,关闭了对话空间,表示作者陈述的内容是毋庸置疑的,不需要和读者进行磋商。然后作者运用承认策略(… *People's Daily* reports … ; … a Jordanian newspaper comments …),分别引用了《人民日报》和约旦报纸的报道,《人民日报》报道中国企业的基础设施项目给约旦当地居民带来了切实的利益,而约旦报纸评论表明中国企业的资金、设备、科技等在约旦地区很受欢迎。众所周知,报纸内容是被新闻从业者证实之后撰写出来的,具有权威性,新闻作者在这里引述了不同国家的新闻报纸评论,打开了对话空间,呈现包容开放的报道立场,同时向读者表明,在开放的话语空间内,多种声音表达的立场却出奇一致,即报纸出处不同而报道内容却相同,这表明中国企业在基础设施建设方面的确给约旦人民带来了实质利益。作者以一个传话者的身份向读者表明,报道内容是客观中立的,话语空间是包容开放的,多种声音不约而同地表达了相同的观点,从而增强了新闻报道的可信性,赢得了读者的信任与支持。

在详述部分,新闻作者运用了大量承认策略(Zhang Shuibao, vice manager of the branch, said …),阐述了完成这个项目的难度之大以及供水系统对约旦人民的帮助。"We are deeply moved by local people visiting us with roast meat and fruits",作者运用词汇"deeply moved"以及"roast meat and fruits"来表明中国人民在"一带一路"建设中的无私奉献,以及约旦人民对此的感激之情。在这里,新闻作者转述部门副经理的话,是因为部门副经理全程参与指导整个工程项目,具有优先发言权,从而增加了转述内容的可信度。新闻作者运用承认策略打开了对话空间,多种声音此起彼伏,展现了项目的规模和困难,以及约旦当地民众对合作项目的赞许和欢迎,让读者有身临其境之感,读者仿佛通过转述话语看到一幅幅画面,映在眼前的就是项目实施过程的画面和约旦人民举着烤肉和水果夹道欢呼的画面。作者由此获得了新闻读者的信任,与新闻读者结成了评价同盟。接着作者运用同样的介入策略向读者陈述了中国给予约旦电力设施建设的支持。作者用事实说明中国在"一带一路"建设中的领导力和影响力,在基础设施建设方面与沿线国家合作,造福当地百姓,从而达到共建共赢的目标。

在解释部分,新闻作者通过支持策略(The newly-signed two projects are also expected to …;Winning these bids shows…)来阐述中国给约旦提供基础设施、能源利用,石油开发等方面支持的原因及结果。中国是"一带一路"建设的倡议者,也是核心力量,有意愿也有信心通过"一带一路"建设拉动沿线国家甚至是整个世界的发展。作者直接肯定转述对象的话语,为转述内容承担一部分责任,与转述对象结成评价联盟,这意味着间接压制其他声音,从而缩小对话空间,目的是得到读者的充分信任,以便与读者形成统一战线,让读者认识到中国是"一带一路"建设的发起者和中坚力量:作为世界上最大发展中国家和人口最多的国家,中国有责任通过自己力量来带动沿线各国发展,这便是中国积极与各国合作,帮助各国建设基础设施的初衷和目的,这也充分体现"一带一路"倡议的宗旨和内涵。

在评论部分,新闻作者运用支持策略(Hu advocates China-Jordan cooperation … as a good example for …)转述胡尚秀的话来阐明中国与约旦两国间合作的示范作用。转述对象胡尚秀表示 Hussein 联合循环发电厂的项目为约旦当地居民提供了超过 1000 个工作岗位,赞扬中国和约旦的合作为沿线国家树立了榜样,这些合作项目通过创造工作岗位和工程采购等方式促进了当地经济增长。作者运用支持策略将被引述的观点看作是正确的,支持并突显这些被引述的观点,某种程度上就模糊并压制了其他观点,从而压缩了对话空间,这样做有可能引起一些读者的反感和质疑,但新闻作者为此愿意承担一部分话语责任。这表明,作者充满信心地认为,通过转述并支持胡尚秀的话,能够赢得大部分读者的认同,这不仅体现了作者自己对转述话语的信任,也表现出作者认为转述话语对读者的影响力足够大可以说服大部分读者。这就是新闻作者对读者心理的揣摩、作者和读者之间的意义磋商,充分体现了支持策略的人际意义。

在背景部分,作者运用单声策略(Guangdong Yudean Group is cooperating with power companies …; China provided around US $1.6 billion in fund for …)来描述该新闻事件的背景、中国政府的相应举措以及后续影响等。作为此阶段话语空间里唯一的声音,作者通过具体数字向读者表明作者陈述内容的真实性毋庸置疑,不受挑战。作者运用了一系列介入策略后,在新闻语篇结尾处,通过单声策略关闭话语空间,这表明作者认为,语篇发展到此处,读者已经接受了作者立场,与读者的评价联盟已经稳固,因此单声策略的人际风险较低(即不容易引起读者排斥)。同时,单声策略突显作者观点,即中国和约旦的合作有前期基础和后续拓展,项目规模不断扩大,合作参与国家日益增多,充分体现了"一带一路"建设的宗旨:国际合作,互利共赢;作为"一带一路"倡议的发起国和主导力量,中国政府为此提供资金保障,彰显负责任大国的国际形象。

设施联通成功的关键之一就是项目的建设和运作方式得到项目参与方的支持,尤其是大国和小国共同参与时能够通过项目实施方式的创新化解小国的顾虑和担忧(宁留甫,2016)。"Chinese enterprises, with their capital, equipment and technology, are popular in Jordan, a Jordanian newspaper comments",此处,语篇利用承认资源(comments),间接引述约旦当地新闻媒体的评论,表现中国企业在当地广受欢迎,获得约旦民众的普遍支持,为基础设施建设的合作提供了民意保障。"Hu Shangxiu, the Hussein project's manager assistant, said, 'Winning these bids shows that Jordan has trust in us.'"语篇直接转述合作项目中方负责人的话语,体现约旦政府对"一带一路"倡议下设施联通的信任。通过转述中国和约旦双方代表的话语,充分扩展话语空间,增强新闻报道的真实感和权威性。随后,语篇通过单声策略,呈现该合作项目为当地百姓带来的切实利益

(The Hussein project has created more than 1,000 jobs for the locals),在封闭的话语空间内,语篇作者是唯一的发声者,该小句的内容被设定为客观事实,无须协商,此合作项目为当地创造超过 1000 个工作岗位,促进当地经济发展,增强当地人民的幸福感,打消关于项目合作的顾虑和担忧。

设施联通的具体合作领域中,应加强能源基础设施互联互通合作,重点建设能源输送管道等基础设施,推进跨境电力和输电通道建设。该语篇报道重点就是约旦国内的能源基础设施建设(Hu advocates China-Jordan cooperation in areas including energy and infrastructure as a good example for bilateral capacity cooperation)。此处,语篇通过支持策略(advocates),突显两国在设施联通方面的合作卓有成效,已成为"一带一路"建设中双边合作的典范,在开放的话语空间内,语篇作者明确支持转述观点,与被转述方建立评价联盟,共同承担话语责任,某种程度上,压制其他声音和立场,收缩了话语空间。与此同时,语篇利用单声策略,报道中国在约旦境内承建的各类项目(A water supply network upgrading project conducted with Chinese aid in Zarqa, Jordan has recently been completed),以及项目的实施效果和对当地人民生活的积极影响(The pipeline can deliver 520 cubic meters of water per hour to meet the needs of half a million residents, who previously could only have three to four hours of water supply a week)。通过单声策略,在封闭的话语空间内,以陈述客观事实的方式,表明两国间合作成果显著,当地百姓享受到了"一带一路"建设带来的切实红利,这是毋庸置疑的,无须就此进行对话协商,语篇作者愿意为该立场承担全责。

基础设施联通的范围广泛,且都要涉及跨境建设,其复杂程度、困难程度都比较大。正如语篇所示,"Zhang Shuibao, vice manager of the branch, said, 'Our workers overcame many difficulties to complete the project. We are deeply moved by local people visiting us with roast meat and fruits.'"通过承认策略(said),语篇直接转述中方承建单位负责人的话语,点明项目建设过程中困难重重,体现出中国工人的敬业精神和专业能力,同时,描述当地百姓对中方工作人员的慰问和关心,突显了"一带一路"建设项目在约旦国内深入人心。

最后,在"一带一路"倡议实施以来,我们与沿线国家签署了一系列基础设施建设工程协议,为设施联通提供政策保障和法律支持。"After fulfilling the add-on cycle power plant contract of Samra's phase II projects in 2010, China's Shandong Electric Power Construction Corp III Electric Power Construction Corp. (SEPCO Ⅲ) again become the EPC contractor …",语篇通过单声资源,报道了中国企业与约旦当地政府签署工程合同,确保设施联通建设顺利实施,既体现了约旦政府和人民对"一带一路"倡议的认可和支持,也

说明中方企业在基础设施建设方面实力雄厚、务实高效,值得信赖。

三、"贸易畅通"语篇的介入策略

"贸易畅通"是"一带一路"建设的重要支柱。"一带一路"建设涵盖许多沿线国家,市场规模和潜力都不可忽视,自"一带一路"倡议实施以来,中方与有关国家和国际组织签署经贸合作协议涵盖自贸区、投资、基础设施、经济合作区、中小企业合作、电子商务等诸多领域,并从 2018 年起举办中国国际进口博览会,与沿线国家合作实施 100 个贸易投资促进项目,未来 5 年为沿线国家提供 10000 个来华研修和培训名额,支持世贸组织和联合国相关机构 20 项贸易投资促进安排等。中国与沿线国家进行贸易交流的同时也就贸易和投资便利化问题进行探讨并做出适当安排,消除贸易壁垒、降低贸易和投资成本、提高区域经济循环速度和质量,实现互利共赢。

在"一带一路"倡议实施过程中,中国与沿线国家进行大量的贸易往来,并制定相应政策来促进贸易发展。例如:跨境电子商务合作,中哈连云港物流合作基地所依托的亚欧跨境货运班列,中巴新合建的"一带一路"农业产业园等。下面以 2017 年 7 月 18 日发表在中国一带一路网上题为"Heilongjiang-Russia trade ties blossom"的新闻为例,阐明介入资源在贸易畅通新闻语篇中的应用策略和人际意义,以

及语类结构中各阶段交际目的如何影响语篇介入策略的韵律
话语模式。新闻原文如下：

Heilongjiang-Russia trade ties blossom

Northeast China's Heilongjiang Province，bordering
Russia，has taken many steps in recent years to boost trade
and business with its neighbor，but it needs to make further
reforms to improve connectivity，experts said on July 17.

Thanks to geographical proximity，Heilongjiang has
been a significant trade partner of Russia，and the China-
proposed "Belt and Road" initiative has also brought the
province into the spotlight.

Heilongjiang is expected to play a bigger role in
enhancing cooperation with Russia's Far East，Bai Ming，a
research fellow at the Chinese Academy of International
Trade and Economic Cooperation，told the *Global Times* on
Monday.

Bilateral trade with Russia surged nearly 42 percent
year-on-year in the first quarter of 2017 to US＄2.67
billion，which accounted for 14 percent of total Russia-China
trade，according to a post on the website of Heilongjiang
provincial government on July 11. The province is China's
busiest in terms of trade with Russia.

In the first five months of 2017, China-Russia trade expanded 33.7 percent year-on-year, reflecting the countries' complementary industrial structures, domestic news site cri. cn reported on July 4, citing data from the General Administration of Customs.

To maintain a steady trade partnership with Russia, Heilongjiang has taken steps to improve connectivity with some major Russian cities along the Trans-Siberian rail route such as Irkutsk and Novosibirsk, which serve as hubs to accelerate trade. Some cities in the northeastern province also unveiled industry restructuring guidelines to attract more Russian investors.

For example, since the beginning of this year, Mudanjiang, a city in the eastern part of Heilongjiang which is located about 200 kilometers from Russia's Ussuriysk, has been actively tapping into the dairy market in the neighboring country. It has also set up seafood-processing factories that handle rising imports from Russia, according to the local government's website.

"Heilongjiang has advantages in agriculture-related industries that can be further explored in cooperating with Russia," Bai said, noting that after the Ukraine crisis, Russia's exports of farm products were affected. China subsequently became a major importer in this segment.

Volatility of the Russian currency has had an impact on border trade in the past few years, but the impact probably eased since the second half of 2016, Jiang Yi, a senior research fellow with the Chinese Academy of Social Sciences, told the *Global Times* on Monday. Although depreciation of the ruble did affect small businesses in the region, this factor only involved a small part of China-Russia trade, he said, noting that the province still faces challenges in strengthening trade ties with Russia.

"Although China-Russia trade has been growing rapidly, few traded goods were produced in the province, so that meant few benefits for local industries," Jiang stressed.

As a traditional industrial base in China, the province has been struggling in terms of GDP growth due to the lack of reforms and sluggish economic restructuring, which will also hinder its trade growth with Russia.

Heilongjiang, together with Northeast China's Liaoning Province and North China's Shanxi Province, was the last three nationwide in terms of GDP growth for a third consecutive year in 2016.

该新闻语场是在"一带一路"倡议下,中国黑龙江和俄罗斯在贸易上的具体成就,并希望通过改革进一步加强贸易合作。语旨是新闻机构和读者,新闻机构是中国一带一路网,它是中国政府对外宣传"一带一路"的官方新闻网站,读者是海内外希望了解"一带一路"建设的各界人士。语式是在网络上以文字形式呈现的新闻话语。该新闻语篇结构各部分依次展开顺序如下:开篇——详述——解释——评论——背景。

在开篇部分,新闻作者运用单声策略撰写新闻标题(Heilongjiang-Russia trade ties blossom),向读者表明黑龙江与俄罗斯之间的贸易关系逐渐加强,揭示了新闻主题,读者通过阅读标题就知道语篇的语场,并产生兴趣去深入解读整个语篇。接着新闻作者运用承认策略(Northeast China's Heilongjiang Province, bordering Russia, has taken many steps in recent years to boost trade and business with its neighbor, but it needs to make further reforms to improve connectivity, experts said on July 17),转述专家们的话语表明虽然黑龙江与俄罗斯之间贸易频繁,但是要实现畅通,还需要进一步改革。因为黑龙江与俄罗斯之间的贸易从宏观上说属于国家间的贸易,作者认为,自己的阐述难以使读者信服,而专门研究两国贸易的专家学者的言论更有说服力,所以新闻作者运用承认策略转述专家学者的话语,展开了对话空间,容纳了多人意见,突显观点的客观公正、真实可靠,争取赢得读者的认可,潜移默化地将自己观点渗入到语篇中,影响读者的阅读立场,从而与读者结成了评价联盟。

在详述部分,新闻作者运用大量承认策略(…, Bai Ming, a research fellow at the Chinese Academy of International Trade and Economic Cooperation, told the *Global Times* on Monday; … according to a post on the website of Heilongjiang provincial government on July 11; … domestic news site cri. cn reported on July 4 …)来阐述 2017年黑龙江和俄罗斯的双边贸易成果。新闻作者引用中国国际贸易经济合作研究院的研究员白明的话语,说明黑龙江希望与俄罗斯远东地区加强进一步合作。因为研究院的研究员是专门分析双方的贸易趋势和贸易价值,所以他的言论具有很强的针对性,新闻作者在这里想向读者传达一个观点,即研究员的专业研究表明,黑龙江与俄罗斯贸易合作加强的趋势是翘首以待的。并且新闻作者引用黑龙江省政府官网上具体数据来阐明2017年中国与俄罗斯的贸易成果。众所周知,政府官网数据更精确、更权威,被引率也更高,不仅中国人民可以看到,甚至是俄罗斯乃至全世界的人民都可以看到。在此,新闻作者运用承认策略向读者展示黑龙江与俄罗斯的贸易关系,扩展了对话空间。除了一如既往采用承认策略,转述专业人士话语使得观点更有权威性,新闻作者还引用大量政府官网数据,使得观点更精确、更真实,受众面也更广,从而悄无声息地将自己观点植入语篇,渗透到读者心里。作者之所以毫无保留地引用政府统计数据,就是为了提高新闻语篇的说服力,打消读者疑虑,驳斥潜在质疑,促使读者认同作者立场。通过承认策略,扩展话语空间,包容各种声音,引用政府数据,体现报道深度,从而烘托出新闻语篇的客观性、公正性、包容性和可靠性,最终赢得读者的信任和认同。紧接着,语篇继续通过承认策略,引用当地政府网站信息,举例说明黑龙江和俄罗斯在具体领域的双边贸易发展。在贸易结构方面,中国与俄罗斯之间的互补性非常明显,中国主要出口制造业领域商品,从俄罗斯进口则包括大量资源型商品(王志远,2016)。语篇此处利用承认策略(according to the local government's website),报道牡丹江市从俄罗斯进口奶制品原材料(… Mudanjiang … has been actively tapping into the dairy market in the neighboring country),以及建立工厂,加工处理从俄罗斯进口的海鲜物资(It has also set up seafood-processing factories that handle rising imports from Russia)。

在解释部分,新闻作者运用支持策略(… noting that after the Ukraine crisis, Russia's exports of farm products were affected. China subsequently became a major importer in this segment)来解释黑龙江与俄罗斯的贸易频繁的原因。影响黑龙江与俄罗斯两方贸易的因素众多,比如地理位置、主打产业、经济政策、结构调整等。新闻作者通过转述并表示支持被引用的观点,表明作者愿意为所引述观点负责。除此之外,新闻作者还运用了反对策略(… but the impact probably eased since the second half of 2016; Although depreciation of the ruble did affect small businesses in the region, this factor only involved a small part of China-Russia trade…)来消除读者的疑虑。影响两国贸易的因素有积极的，也有消极的。新闻作者阐述俄罗斯货币汇率的变动对两国贸易产生很大影响，读者会推断卢布贬值将使两国的贸易量缩减，在这里作者揣摩到了读者心思，然后运用反对策略否定了一种潜在观点（即读者的推断），表示自从 2016 年下半年以来，货币汇率的影响就已经降低，而且汇率变动对两国贸易的影响甚微，根本改变不了总体趋势。通过支持策略和反对策略，话语空间收缩：支持策略突显引述观点，建立作者与引述对象的立场联盟，淡化其他声音；反对策略首先唤起潜在观点，引起读者共鸣，获得读者信任，然后否定读者推断，突显作者立场，展现缜密逻辑和全面考虑，赢得读者认可，建立与读者的评价联盟。

在评论部分，新闻作者继续运用支持策略和反对策略（"Although China-Russia trade has been growing rapidly, few traded goods were produced in the province, so that meant few benefits for local industries," Jiang stressed)来阐述黑龙江与俄罗斯贸易面临的挑战。在"一带一路"倡议下，中俄贸易不断加强，无疑促进了两国经济增长。但作者没有一味渲染其巨大影响力，而是通过转述指出黑龙江只是中国与俄罗斯贸易的中转站，少有产品产自黑龙江本地，这对当地产业发展帮助有限。此处，新闻作者转述并支持研究员蒋毅的话语,主动与他建立态度同盟,压制其他观点,收缩话语空间,与此同时,通过反对策略,暗示另一种观点(也是读者可能的推断):中俄贸易迅速发展,很多产品源自黑龙江,当地产业获益巨大。然后提出相反观点,否定潜在的推断,缩小话语空间,由此向读者表明:作者洞察了读者的心思,作者比读者更了解新闻事件的前因后果,作者纠正了读者的推断。通过这些介入策略,作者旨在赢得读者信任,与读者建立评价同盟,说服读者接受语篇立场。

在背景阶段,新闻作者运用单声策略陈述了黑龙江自身经济发展背景(Heilongjiang, …, was the last three nationwide in terms of GDP growth for a third consecutive year in 2016)。黑龙江、辽宁和山西连续三年 GDP 增长率在全国所有省份中是最低的,反映出黑龙江急需推动与俄罗斯的贸易发展,为省内的产业复兴注入活力,同时也面临诸多现实困难。通过单声策略,关闭对话空间,只呈现作者自己声音,表明所述内容为既成事实,无可争议。这说明,在新闻语篇最后阶段,作者认为已经赢得了读者信任,巩固了与读者的评价同盟,无须借助外部声音影响读者立场,突显自己声音足以增强语篇的说服力。

四、"资金融通"语篇的介入策略

"资金融通"为"一带一路"建设提供了重要资金保障。

"一带一路"沿线多数国家经济基础薄弱,地缘政治错综复杂,因此中国金融领域的支持力度加强,促进沿线国家基础设施等重大项目的建设。其中,中国国家开发银行、丝绸基金等是支持企业"走出去"的主力军,而且中国还打造市场化、多层次的融资体系,严格控制资金的风险评估与防范,为"一带一路"倡议的宏伟蓝图增色添彩。

在"一带一路"倡议实施过程中,中国为沿线国家提供大量的资金支持,例如:中国出口信用保险公司与南非标准银行签署框架合作协议,香港将为亚投行项目准备专项基金 1000 万美元,中欧共同投资基金正式成立并投入实质性运作等。下面以 2017 年 11 月 20 日刊登在中国一带一路网上题为 "Belt and Road investment beckons"的新闻为例,阐明介入资源在资金融通新闻语篇中的应用策略和人际意义,以及语类结构中各阶段交际目的如何影响语篇介入策略的韵律话语模式。新闻原文如下:

Belt and Road investment beckons

A recently released report says countries in eastern Africa have the potential to become major destinations of Chinese outbound investment under the Belt and Road Initiative.

These countries, according to "Belt & Road: Opportunities & Risk—The prospects and perils of building

China's New Silk Road", a report by Baker McKenzie and Silk Road Associates, are Kenya, Tanzania, Ethiopia, Djibouti and Egypt.

The report says underdeveloped infrastructure such as energy and transportation will attract increased Chinese investment to the continent in the next five years. In addition, by 2025, benefits from Belt and Road will spread substantially to other sectors due to improved infrastructure, eventually attracting private players, especially in such nascent sectors as technology, telecommunications and manufacturing.

"East Africa is a more integral part of (Belt and Road) owing to Djibouti's ports, Ethiopia's manufacturing and the region's existing plans to connect rail, road and energy networks," says the report. Current investments range from standard gauge railways in Kenya and Ethiopia to planned projects in Tanzania and Uganda.

The World Bank is convinced that the continent needs $93 billion per year to bridge its infrastructure gap. Moreover, a report by Ernst & Young says China is already the single largest contributor to foreign direct investment to the continent and has invested in 293 projects in Africa since 2005, totaling investment outlay of $66.4 billion.

The Baker McKenzie report says Egypt offers a significant opportunity for Chinese companies that will need to collaborate with local players and multilateral banks to surmount big challenges.

"Key opportunities will be transactions related to major projects in the power and infrastructure sector and related financing. China's construction of power plants and transmission lines in East Africa will be a game changer for local industry. Port connectivity will also improve significantly in the next five years," the report says.

It estimates that Belt and Road projects will see at least $350 billion in investment in new projects in countries participating in the initiative. While infrastructure development has been the primary Belt and Road driver, the Baker McKenzie report says other sectors will emerge to play a role.

There will be increased entry of Chinese smart phone and household electronic brands to Africa as they look to repeat their success in Southeast Asia and South Asia, the report says.

"Chinese investments in technology, media and telecommunications across the region, alongside rising incomes, will contribute to a surge in demand for smart phones and internet-based services. Moreover, China's leading private firms have the cash flow to fund their expansion into (Belt and Road) markets. They are not reliant on government funding and will leverage their distribution partners to grow."

Regarding consumer goods and retail, the report says China's investments in roads, railways and power across the continent will support household incomes and spur the already growing retail and food sectors.

Calling it a multi-decade initiative that will reshape China's commercial engagement with the world, the report says that although Belt and Road will connect China and Europe, it "differs in that the Road passes through Southeast Asia, South Asia, the Middle East and East Africa, a region that is home to 42 percent of the world's population and 25 percent of its GDP, excluding China."

Stanley Jia, the chief Beijing representative of Baker McKenzie, is confident that Belt and Road "is and will continue to be the most important and impactful macroeconomic undertaking in the world, for at least the next 10 years."

Currently there are already more than 1,700 Belt and Road projects either completed or in development. As more infrastructure projects are completed，more Chinese private companies will want to participate and will subsequently offer huge opportunities for local and international partners in a wide variety of sectors.

While Belt and Road was seen at its inception as predominantly the reserve of Chinese state-owned enterprises，funded by Chinese banks and staffed by Chinese workers，the sheer scale and ambition of the initiative means there will be plenty of opportunities for those local and multinational companies that can work hand in hand with Chinese organizations for mutual benefit，particularly as this second wave of Chinese investments arrives.

　　该新闻语场是在"一带一路"倡议下，中国在对东非国家能源、交通、科技、通讯、媒体等领域投资巨大，推动当地基础设施建设，充分践行了"一带一路"倡议的目标与宗旨。语旨是新闻机构和读者，新闻机构是中国一带一路官网，它是中国政府对外宣传"一带一路"的官方新闻网站，读者是海内外希望了解"一带一路"的各界人士。语式是通过网络以文字形式呈现的新闻话语。该新闻语篇结构各部分依次展开顺序如下：开篇——详述——解释——评论——背景。

　　在新闻开篇部分，新闻作者运用单声策略（Belt and Road investment beckons）呈现新闻标题，言简意赅，吸引读者兴趣。作者认为此新闻事实是毋庸置疑的,无须和读者进行磋商,而且作者认为在新闻开篇阶段有必要以此事实开场,定下评价基调,让读者明白中国为"一带一路"建设准备了充足资金,完全有经济实力实施"一带一路"倡议。作者运用承认策略,以间接投射的方式(A recently released report says …)引出新闻语篇的导语,指出在"一带一路"倡议下,东非国家有望成为中国境外投资的主要目的地。在此,作者引用官方报告内容,打开对话空间,表明该报告只是一家之言,暗示存在其他立场,向读者呈现客观公正的话语空间,愿意与读者进行态度磋商,从而赢得读者尊重,与读者初步建立评价同盟,促使读者继续阅读新闻,留在话语空间内,以便在语篇随后阶段说服读者,最终让读者认可中国在发展"资金融通"方面的雄厚实力和坚定决心。

在详述部分,新闻作者运用承认策略(The report says underdeveloped infrastructure such as … ; … says the report …)转述媒体报告,详细阐述在"一带一路"倡议下,中国对东非国家的能源和交通等基础设施的投资前景,以及对科技、通讯和制造业等新兴产业的深远影响。在此,新闻作者以媒体机构作为转述对象,是因为作者认为关于"资金融通"的新闻语篇,很多细节涉及金钱交易,西方读者眼里,政府官员只负责政策制定和沟通,不能参与金融交易,而经济学家的话语有时过于专业,宣传效果不佳,而银行高管往往顾及金融机密,不愿意透露敏感信息,因此媒体机构自然就成了最佳转述对象。作者通过转述媒体话语,打开了对话空间,引入了多种声音,唤起了多种立场观点,增强了新闻语篇的客观性和全面性,从而获得了读者的信任和认同。

在解释部分,新闻作者运用支持策略(The World Bank is convinced that the continent needs $93 billion per year to …；It estimates that Belt and Road projects will see at least $350 billion in investment in…)来阐述"一带一路"投资的前因后果。中国对东非国家投资的原因之一是这些国家的基础设施建设缺乏资金,需要中国牵头,联合沿线国家共同建立融资渠道。与此同时,"一带一路"建设为东非国家带来投资后,不仅推动了基础设施建设,而且促进了当地其他产业的发展,如科技、通信、制造业、食品和服务业等,也为中国企业的生存和发展提供了契机。新闻作者在此运用支持策略,主动为转述话语承担责任,缩小对话空间,意在向读者表明"一带一路"倡议并不是要求中国一味地去帮助沿线国家,而是通过合作,取长补短,互利共赢,从而消除了读者的疑虑,将读者拉到了自己的一方,以便之后与新闻读者结成评价同盟。

在评论部分,新闻作者运用支持策略(Stanley Jia, the chief Beijing representative of Baker Mckenzie, is confident that …)和反对策略(… although Belt and Road will connect China and Europe, it differs in that the Road passes through Southeast Asia, …)向读者表明中国"一带一路"建设是未来10年影响力最深远的全球经济活动,其资金融通措施会带动

各个产业发展,推动亚洲和非洲的经济融合、产业合作,变革世界金融运作模式,改变中国参与世界贸易的方式。"一带一路"两端连接中国和欧洲,但更重要的是沿线的东南亚、南亚、中东和东非等国家。此处,作者揣摩读者心理,认为读者可能推断"一带一路"重点是中国和欧洲的合作发展,于是作者运用转折词汇(although)向读者表明,作者知道读者的推断,并理解读者推断的理由,同时指出读者的推断是错误的,而事实是"一带一路"是面向全球的经济倡议:沿线部分国家占世界总人口的 42%,占全球 GDP 的 25%,这还不包括中国,足以体现"一带一路"对世界经济的影响力。新闻作者还转述并支持 Baker Mckenzie 机构的北京代表 Stanley Jia 的话语,表示"一带一路"倡议将在未来 10 年内对世界经济产生重要影响。该转述内容可能会引起一些读者的排斥,认为作者夸大了"一带一路"倡议的影响力,所以作者运用支持策略,压缩了对话空间,主动为转述话语负责,并与转述对象建立评价同盟。通过转述并支持 Stanley Jia 的话语,作者充满信心地认为,能够赢得大部分读者的认同,这不仅体现了作者对"一带一路"倡议巨大影响力的肯定,也体现了作者认为 Stanley Jia 话语对读者的影响力足够大到可以说服大部分读者。可见,作者不断揣摩读者心理,通过支持策略影响读者的阅读立场,与读者建立评价联盟,充分体现了介入策略的人际意义。

在背景部分,作者运用单声策略(Currently there are already more than 1,700 Belt and Road projects either completed or in development. While Belt and Road was seen at its inception as predominantly the reserve of Chinese state-owned enterprises, …）阐述"一带一路"倡议下,中国在资金融通方面的努力和后续影响。过去"一带一路"项目多数由中国国有企业牵头,资金来自中国国有银行,员工也来自中国,目前已有1700多个项目完成或在实施中,但是随着沿线各国基础设施建设推进,更多中国私营企业、沿线当地企业和跨国公司会参与"一带一路"建设,促进各产业的国际合作,本着携手共进、互利共赢的精神,为各类"一带一路"项目吸引更多投资,注入更多资金,推动资金融通发展。在此,新闻作者关闭对话空间,为话语承担全部责任,向读者表明自己对"一带一路"倡议下资金融通的发展充满信心,说明作者认为在语篇结尾处与读者的立场联盟基本稳固,无须借助外界声音说服读者,通过单声策略直接阐明作者立场,巩固与读者间的评价同盟。

五、"民心相通"语篇的介入策略

"民心相通"是"一带一路"建设坚实的民意基础和社会根基。传承和弘扬丝绸之路友好合作精神,广泛开展文化交流、学术往来、人才交流、媒体合作、青年和妇女交往、志愿者服务等,从而深化中国与沿线各国的双边或多边合作(乔榛,2018)。在推动"一带一路"建设过程中,我国在教育、文化、科技、旅游、卫生、救灾援助和减贫等人文交流合作方面,做了大量工作,为"一带一路"建设营造了良好的舆论氛围,赢得了沿线民众的支持。与此同时,"一带一路"沿线国家也兴建了许多"中国文化中心"、孔子学院等教科文化机构。总之,"一带一路"倡议加强了沿线国家人民的友好往来,增进了相互了解和传统友谊,为开展区域合作奠定了广泛的群众基础。

随着"一带一路"倡议的实施,各国的文化交流诸如旅游热、汉语热、孔子学院等日益频繁,中国在民心相通方面也采取了重大举措,例如:卡塔尔与中国签署互免签证协定,"一带一路"沿线国际游规模占全球旅游七成,中国向柬埔寨援助现代化医疗设备,派遣医疗组提供技术支持等。下面以2017年6月26日发表在中国一带一路网上题为"Chinese, Ukrainian university chiefs discuss cooperation in higher education"的新闻为例,阐明介入资源在民心相通的新闻语篇中的应用策略和人际意义,以及语类结构中各阶段交际目的如何影响该语篇介入策略的韵律话语模式。新闻原文如下:

Chinese, Ukrainian university chiefs discuss cooperation in higher education

The chiefs of 36 major Chinese and Ukrainian universities held a roundtable forum here on Friday to discuss cooperation in higher education and share their experiences.

The discussion, which was held at the Kiev Taras Shevchenko National University, brought together 62 presidents and chancellors of Chinese and Ukrainian universities.

While addressing the forum, Peng Long, president of Beijing Foreign Studies University (BFSU), spoke highly of China-Ukraine higher education cooperation, noting that there are good opportunities to further enhance it.

"The prospects for the development of our cooperation have a good background and I hope that we will manage to build bridges of our cooperation even more efficiently," Peng said.

In the framework of the Belt and Road Initiative, the Ukrainian Centre was set up in the BFSU in June 2016, Peng said, noting that eight students are currently learning the Ukrainian language at the educational facility.

Besides, the BFSU has participated in the exhibition titled "Ukrainian Traditional Culture and Painting", which was held in November last year in Beijing, he said.

At the forum in Kiev, the BFSU plans to further deepen its partnership with Ukrainian universities, signing cooperation agreements with Ukraine's National Linguistic

University and several other educational establishments, Peng added.

Moreover, Rui Zhiyuan, president of Lanzhou University of Technology spoke highly of the forum, noting that his university is already reaping fruits from cooperation with Ukrainian partners.

"In 2015-2016, we received scholarship programs for student exchanges in five directions, including such areas as material knowledge, welding and construction," Rui said.

"We cooperate with Kharkiv Polytechnic Institute, the National Metallurgical Academy of Ukraine, Kiev University of Construction and Architecture and Ivano-Frankivsk National Technical University of Oil And Gas," he said.

Chinese and Ukrainian universities have witnessed frequent student exchanges. In 2016, a total of 3,552 Chinese students studied in Ukraine, while Chinese universities have trained 2,896 Ukrainian students.

Local experts are confident that those exchanges will further deepen, in particular, due to the rising popularity of Chinese culture and language in Ukraine.

Currently, there are five Confucius Institutes and a Confucius Classroom in the East European country, where hundreds of Ukrainians are learning Chinese. Besides, many universities across Ukraine are offering a range of Mandarin courses for their students.

Gennady Pivnyak, Vice President of the Union of Rectors of Ukraine, said that his university has already benefited from cooperation with Chinese partners.

"Our university has sufficient experience of cooperation with Chinese universities and we have a center for learning Chinese," said Pivnyak, who is also a president of the National Mining University in Dnipro city in central Ukraine.

He added that the roundtable meeting between the chiefs of Chinese and Ukrainian universities will help to further deepen the partnership.

"Today is a very bright day, and we will be able to sign the agreements we need in the sphere of energy cooperation. We are interested in cooperation with Beijing University of Technology, Lanzhou University of Technology, and Lanzhou University," Pivnyak said.

Although cooperation between Chinese and Ukrainian universities is flourishing, the chiefs of the educational establishments of the two countries are convinced that the potential of such cooperation is still not fully tapped.

VilBakirov, president of the Kharkiv National University in eastern Ukraine, said that the roundtable forum in Kiev is an important platform to establish new links between cooperating institutions and create new higher education programs between China and Ukraine.

"First of all, I want to stress the great importance of this forum in terms of scope and tasks. We have not yet fully utilized the enormous opportunities that Ukraine and China have. I am deeply convinced that this forum will allow us to make cooperation broader and deeper,"Bakirov said.

The forum, which was opened by visiting Chinese Minister of Education Chen Baosheng, his Ukrainian counterpart Liliya Grynevych, and Chinese Ambassador to Ukraine Du Wei, marked the second meeting of Chinese and Ukrainian university chiefs. The first forum was held in 2012.

　　该新闻语场是来自中国和乌克兰 36 所高校校长参加一个圆桌论坛,讨论两国高等教育合作,分享成功经验,展望未来发展。该语场肯定了"一带一路"倡议下沿线各国教育合作实现了飞跃发展,五通目标之一的民心相通取得了实质性突破。语旨是新闻机构和读者,新闻机构是中国一带一路官网,它是中国政府对外发布"一带一路"新闻的官方网站,读者是希望了解"一带一路"倡议的海内外各界人士。语式是通过网络以文字形式呈现的新闻话语。该新闻语篇结构各部分依次展开顺序如下：开篇——详述——解释——评论——背景。

在开篇部分中，新闻作者运用单声策略撰写新闻标题和导语（The chiefs of 36 major Chinese and Ukrainian universities held a roundtable forum here on Friday to discuss cooperation in higher education and share their experiences)，向读者客观报道新闻事件的基本要素。此处，作者运用单声策略，关闭对话空间，用自己声音向读者传达新闻事实。可见，新闻作者认为导语内容是客观事实，毋庸置疑，无须引述外界声音表现语篇的客观立场，然而，即使在如此看似陈述事实的报道中，我们也能感受到新闻作者的态度。"chiefs"和"major"说明圆桌论坛参与者是两国主要大学的领导人，体现他们在高等教育领域的权威性，"discuss"和"share"表现参与者彼此尊重、平等协商、互相学习的论坛氛围，"experiences"说明参与者在高校合作领域具有前期基础，经验丰富，这些词汇暗示该论坛基于前期两国大学的合作成果，是一个承前启后、继往开来的事件，参与者是高校合作领域的开拓者和领导者，对未来的发展起到决定性作用。新闻作者在封闭话语空间内，通过单声策略，展现新闻事实，营造客观中立的报道立场和真实性，同时运用词汇手段，潜移默化地把自己态度植入语篇，影响读者的阅读立场，引导读者认同作者观点。

在详述部分，新闻作者运用承认策略（"The prospects for the development of our cooperation … ," Peng said. In the framework of the Belt and Road Initiative, the Ukrainian Centre was set up in the BFSU in June 2016，Peng said …）通过直接转述和间接转述北京外国语大学校长彭龙的话语，向读者阐述了中乌高等教育合作的举措、成果、重要性和发展前景。在此，新闻作者通过话语投射而不是直接陈述，旨在向读者表明这是北外校长观点而非自己主观意见，进而撇清了自己的责任。北外校长是新闻事件当事人，引用他的话语增强了转述内容的可信度，使得新闻语篇更有说服力。通过北外校长的话语，读者获悉"一带一路"倡议下，北外与乌克兰的文化交流初见成效，建立了乌克兰语言中心，举办了乌克兰传统文化绘画展等，读者由此感受到中国在促进民心相通方面的努力和效果。新闻作者运用承认策略扩大对话空间，引述外部声音，并与之保持距离，暗示其他声音，显示客观公正的报道立场，赢得读者尊重，为随后建立与读者的评价联盟奠定互信基础。

在解释部分，新闻作者运用支持策略（Rui Zhiyuan, president of Lanzhou University of Technology spoke highly of the forum，noting that …; Local experts are confident that …）解释中乌大学合作论坛举办的原因和影响。在此，新闻作者通过转述并支持兰州理工大学校长芮志远的话语，阐述了"一带一路"倡议下，中乌两国在高等教育领域的合作成果:两国间互派交换生数量与日俱增,合作院校逐渐增加和教育领域逐步扩展,这也是举办此次合作论坛的原因之一,即总结巩固合作成果,推进深化文化交流。此外,通过转述并支持乌克兰当地专家话语,表明召开此次论坛将促进中国语言和文化在乌克兰的推广,吸引更多乌克兰人学习汉语,促使当地大学开办孔子学院和普通话课程。作者在解释阶段运用支持策略,表明态度,支持转述对象的观点,淡化并压制其他立场,收缩对话空间,作者通过突显与自己立场一致的转述内容,主动与转述对象结成评价联盟,影响读者阅读立场,引导读者加入立场同盟并接受作者观点:中乌两国大学合作硕果累累,值此时机,举办圆桌论坛,巩固成果,总结经验,展望未来,为深化合作集思广益,规划蓝图。

在评论部分,新闻作者运用反对策略和支持策略(Although cooperation … is flourishing, the chiefs … are convinced that the potential of such cooperation is still not fully tapped)向读者表明,虽然中乌两国合作日益加强,但是两国高校校长们认为合作潜力依然未被充分开发。新闻作者此处的介入策略充分体现了与读者的态度磋商和人际意义,首先通过"Although"陈述一个观点(即中乌两国的合作日益加强),并以此为基础进行随后的逻辑推断,引导读者把此观点默认为既定事实,然后作者暗示读者持有的潜在观点(即随着中乌合作日益加强,合作潜力已经被充分挖掘),接着作者运用支持策略间接转述两国大学校长们的话语,借他们之口,否定读者持有的潜在观点,并表达与之相反的观点(即两国合作潜力依然未被充分开发)。可见,新闻作者通过反对策略,引导读者接受某一观点为既定事实,在此基础上,展现全面考虑和缜密逻辑,否定读者可能的推断(因此收缩对话空间),说服读者接受作者的推断,建立与读者的立场联盟,然后,通过支持策略,突显转述观点,压制和淡化其他观点,进一步收缩对话空间,巩固与读者的立场联盟。

最后在背景部分,新闻作者运用单声策略(The forum, which was opened by visiting Chinese Minister of Education Chen Baosheng …)表明此类合作论坛已举办两届,早在2012年中乌两国大学领导层就会晤商讨合作事宜。在此,新闻作者关闭了对话空间,用自己声音陈述相关背景,体现"一带一路"倡议下,两国早已认识到高等教育合作的重要性,并在2012年就举办第一届合作论坛,此次圆桌论坛旨在总结已有成果,规划未来发展,为两国进一步合作奠定基础。作者运用单声策略,表明作者认为所述背景信息是既定事实,毋庸置疑,愿意为此承担全部责任。作者在封闭话语空间内,以2012年首届合作论坛为背景,对比眼前新闻事件,引导读者接受语篇立场:中乌两国的教育合作已有五年历史,两国大学领导层高度重视合作成果和发展前景,通过再次举办论坛,回顾合作成果,增进互信了解,挖掘合作潜能。

通过对"一带一路""五通"发展对外新闻的语篇介入策略分析,我们发现这些新闻虽然语场不同,但有一个相似规律,就是新闻语篇随着各阶段交际目的变化,介入话语策略在单声,承认,支持、反对之间不断切换,话语空间总体上呈现从封闭到打开,从扩展到收缩,最后到封闭的变化规律,形成一种韵律话语模式,为对外宣传"一带一路"倡议建构了开放包容、伸缩有序的对话空间:收缩对话空间,旨在突显我国与沿线国家在"五通"发展上的努力和成就,扩展对话空间,旨在营造客观中立的新闻报道立场。最终,潜移默化中新闻作者与读者结成态度同盟,对新闻事件达成一致的正面评价立场,推动"一带一路"倡议深入人心,促进"五通"目标顺利实现。

第六章 "一带一路"对外
新闻态度策略定量分析

本章首先根据 White 新闻语类结构模型,统计出"一带一路"对外新闻中态度资源的分布情况。然后,据此分析态度韵律在小句层面和语篇结构中的发展模式,揭示其修辞说服功能。

一、态度资源的分布规律

根据语类结构的特征对"一带一路"对外新闻的五部分态度策略进行定量分析,统计出"一带一路"对外新闻语篇态度资源分布数据(表 6-1),以及态度资源在语篇中的分布趋势(图 6-1)。

表中数据显示,态度资源分布在各个语步。其中,出现次数最多的是详述语步(565 次),其次是解释语步(538 次)。才能(522 次)是使用数量最高的态度资源。邵斌、蔡颖莹和余晓燕(2018)在分析西方媒体对"一带一路"的英语报道时提出,语义韵最能体现评价和态度,对于揭示媒体的评价态度具

表 6-1 "一带一路"对外新闻态度资源分布

态度资源		新闻语篇								
		开篇部分		详述部分		解释部分		背景部分		评论部分	
		数量	比例/%	数量	比例/%	数量	比例/%	数量	比例/%	数量	比例/%
情感	高兴	0	0.00	0	0.00	3	0.56	0	0.00	27	14.92
	安全	7	2.27	13	2.30	10	1.86	9	1.81	23	12.70
	满意	14	4.53	21	3.71	14	2.60	12	2.42	40	22.10
	合计	21	6.80	34	6.01	27	5.02	21	4.23	90	49.72
判断	规范	39	12.62	81	14.34	36	6.69	39	7.86	7	3.87
	才能	126	40.78	243	43.01	68	12.64	67	13.51	18	9.95
	坚韧	58	18.77	104	18.41	61	11.34	34	6.85	13	7.18
	真实	0	0.00	0	0.00	10	1.86	5	1.02	0	0.00
	得体	10	3.23	15	2.65	27	5.02	27	5.44	0	0.00
	合计	233	75.40	443	78.41	202	37.55	172	34.68	38	21.00
鉴赏	反应	6	1.94	14	2.48	108	20.07	113	22.78	21	11.60
	构成	18	5.83	33	5.84	59	10.97	52	10.48	8	4.42
	价值	31	10.03	41	7.26	142	26.39	138	27.83	24	13.26
	合计	55	17.80	88	15.58	309	57.43	303	61.09	53	29.28
总计		309	100.00	565	100.00	538	100.00	496	100.00	181	100.00

有特殊意义。我们也认为,单个态度资源孤立存在,无法充分体现其修辞功能,而多个态度资源互相联合,彼此呼应,在语篇中形成某种态度韵律后,能更有效地达到语篇修辞目的。因此,本章研究重点是态度韵律的修辞功能,将从三个说服功能视角,探讨三种态度韵律的修辞意义。

本章首先运用评价理论态度系统,阐明三种态度韵律的实现形式,然后根据表 6-1 具体分析态度资源在小句层面的

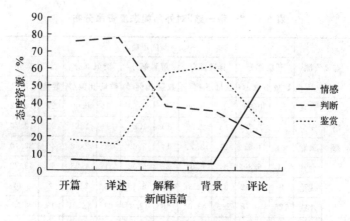

图 6-1 "一带一路"对外新闻态度资源趋势

发展模式,揭示其如何通过渗透型韵律、主导型韵律以及增强型韵律,实现情感说服、人品说服和逻辑说服。

Martin 和 White(2005)用表"可能"的情态在句子中展开的方式来说明渗透型的韵律结构。例如:**I suppose** he **might possibly** have, **mightn't** he?

这种情态可以表现为第一人称现在时的心理过程(I suppose),进而体现在情态词和情态状语上(might possibly),最后又以反意疑问尾句的形式再度重申(mightn't),渗透型韵律贯穿于整个句子当中。

增强型韵律结构可以通过反复、下级修饰(submodification)、感叹句结构、最高级等形式体现,例如:**What an** amazing album. "Love Struck Baby" starts it off and is one of their **most** famous songs. "Testify" is one of the great**est** songs Stevie ever did.

最后一类是主导型韵律结构，Martin（2005）认为，Halliday 提出的语气成分在小句中起着主导作用，而剩余成分在这个域中有着和语气成分同样的意义。例如：If you do**n't** get **no** publicity，you do**n't** get **no** people at the fight. If you do**n't** get **no** bums on seats you do**n't** get paid … Anyway I enjoy it.

在渗透型韵律结构中，韵律的体现是随机的，它会在任何能够显现的地方显现出来；增强型韵律结构牵涉到扩大，它类似于音量的提升，语篇的情感意义在语篇语境中得到回应；主导型韵律结构是将其本身的意义与所辖范围内其他意义相关联（Martin & White，2005），如图 6-2 所示。

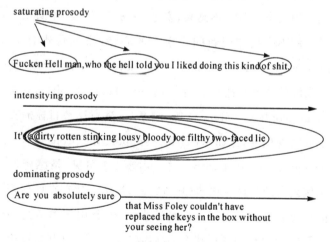

图 6-2 三种韵律体现示意图（Martin & White，2005：24）

同时,他们提出语篇层面也存在着这样的结构。本章目的就是分析态度资源如何构建态度韵律模式,揭示"一带一路"对外新闻语篇中态度韵律的内在运作方式和修辞策略的实现机制。

二、态度资源的情感说服策略

情感说服策略是指唤起读者情感共鸣,以情动人,以达到说服目的。新闻语篇激发读者某种情感,引导读者接受作者植入语篇的观点和立场,这可以通过态度系统中的情感资源,构建渗透型态度韵律得以实现。

情感系统揭示人的内心感受,Martin 和 White(2005)将情感分为三类:高兴/不高兴,安全/不安全,满意/不满意。其中,高兴/不高兴体现新闻当事人的心情,常见句式有 I am glad to visit…, He was pleased to notice… 等;安全/不安全涉及人际信任和理想信念,例如 China believes that…, Both sides are confident about… 等;满意/不满意反映目标的支持力度或实现程度,比如 We firmly support the project…, The president is satisfied with… 等。由表 6-1 可见,情感资源运用比例最高的是评论语步(49.72%),该语步旨在点评新闻事件的社会意义和对当事人的情感影响等,其中频率最高的子资源是满意(22.10%),其次是高兴(14.92%)。同时,评论语步中,最显著的态度韵律模式是渗透型,Martin 和 White

(2005)指出,渗透型韵律模式中,韵律是随机出现的,即在任何部分都会显现出来(图 6-3)。

Xi said he is glad that all the consensuses reached by the two sides … China supports Namibia in further developing itself and is willing to strengthen communication and coordination…, Xi said. Geingob said the two sides have been working together on the basis of mutual trust for a long time … Namibia firmly upholds the one-China policy, and think positively of the Belt and Road Initiative, believing the initiative is beneficial to connectivity …, Geingob said.

图 6-3 渗透型态度韵律

图 6-3 中共有 7 处情感资源,均为显性积极的评价词汇,glad(高兴)和 mutual trust(安全)体现新闻当事人对双方合作的认可,supports(满意)和 is willing to(满意)反映他们对中纳两国未来的发展持乐观和满意态度,upholds(满意),thinks positively of(满意)和 believing(安全)表现新闻当事人支持中国国策,积极参与"一带一路"建设。这 7 个情感词语分散在评论语步的各个小句中,形成渗透型韵律模式,彰显了两国领导人为实现共同发展而做出的巨大努力。可见,作者引用两国领导人话语,点评"一带一路"和两国之间的合作时,交替使用所有的情感资源,说明纳米比亚领导人认识到该倡议是"互利共赢"的,愿意扩大与中国的合作,推动"一带一路"建设。此评价姿态通过渗透型态度韵律弥漫在评论语步中,营造出愉快和谐、齐心协力、充满信心的情感氛围,不断激发读者的积极情感,影响读者的阅读立场,潜移默化中建立作者与读者的评价同盟,实现情感说服的修辞策略。

三、态度资源的人品说服策略

人品说服是指塑造说话者品格和威望,以德服人,赢得读者信赖,实现说服目的。新闻语篇树立新闻人物个人形象,突显德才和诚信,促使读者接受语篇立场。这可以通过态度系统中的判断资源,构建主导型态度韵律得以实现。

判断资源分为社会评判和社会约束。社会评判的标准是伦理道德,内含 3 个变量:规范、才能和坚韧;社会约束是基于法律规约的态度资源,包括 2 个变量:真实和得体。表 6-1 显示,判断资源常见于详述语步(78.41%)和开篇语步(75.40%)。开篇语步是新闻语篇的人际意义核心,奠定语篇整体评价基调,详述语步是开篇语步的语义扩展,两语步的态度评价模式基本一致,都以才能为主(40.78%,43.01%),例如:Two leaders call on enhancing … 等,其次是坚韧(18.77%,18.41%),例如:China is dedicated to … 等。态度韵律模式也都以主导型为主,Martin 和 White(2005)表示,主导型韵律模式中,语篇围绕中心评价意义展开,从不同方面与之响应(图 6-4)。

图 6-4 中共有 7 处判断资源,均为隐性的积极评价词汇,通过描述习近平的一系列主张和愿景,向读者展现其睿智实干和胸怀天下的形象,例如标题中:Xi calls for strengthening cooperation。作为合作的发起人,习近平要求加强与东北亚

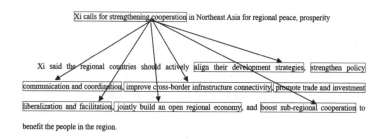

图 6-4 主导型态度韵律

国家的合作以维护地区的和平与繁荣,可见其远见卓识;他深知中国与东亚的合作必然是互利互惠和双赢的结果,有利于实现共同发展。这 7 处判断资源以标题为核心,构成主导型韵律模式,反映了中国和东北亚领导人积极沟通政策,相互借鉴,共同维护地区的安稳和传统友谊。作者在标题中直接点明要义,通过隐性判断资源表现习近平的卓越才能,并以此主导整个语篇的评价态度。在详述语步中,继续利用判断资源中的才能变量,6 例资源来响应标题的评价立场,分别从协调发展策略、加强政策沟通、提高设施联通、推动贸易投资、共建区域经济、促进区域合作 6 个方面体现习近平对"一带一路"沿线国家的支持和帮助,即各国合作,共享成果,构建人类命运共同体,造福全球未来。

借助主导型态度韵律,新闻作者在详述语步中通过判断资源树立习近平作为国家领导人正直无私,勇于担当的高尚品格。对读者而言,习近平的真知灼见体现其人格魅力,犹如音乐旋律,贯穿于详述语步,读者对其敬佩之情油然而生,信任其话语内容,支持其话语立场。新闻语篇由此实现人品说服的修辞策略。

四、态度资源的逻辑说服策略

逻辑说服策略是指通过谋篇布局,强调客观事实和逻辑关联,以理服人,达到说服目的。新闻语篇以清晰连贯的顺序,罗列事实,体现各命题间逻辑关系,帮助读者理解语篇结构和内容,增强语篇立场的说服力。这可以通过态度系统中的鉴赏资源,构建增强型态度韵律得以实现。

鉴赏资源分为反应、构成和价值,其中反应表现事物的质量和影响,例如:The cooperation between two sides is appealing … 等;构成反映事物的细节和复杂性,例如:It was a long-term, high-level and sustainable plan … 等;价值体现事物的社会属性,例如:China's practices can be valuable to the rest of the world … 等。如表 6-1 所示,鉴赏资源使用频率较高是背景语步(61.09%)和解释语步(57.43%)。背景语步旨在提供新闻要素的背景材料,介绍新闻事件的发展脉络,或对比同类事件;解释语步是描述新闻事件的前因后果,可见,两语步的交际目的与逻辑说服策略基本一致。两语步的态度资源分布规律类似,频率最高的是价值(27.83%,26.39%),其次是反应(22.78%,20.07%),态度韵律也都以增强型模式为主。Martin 和 White(2005)表示,增强型韵律模式中,评价态度层层递进,逐步加强,韵律音量不断提高(如图 6-5)。

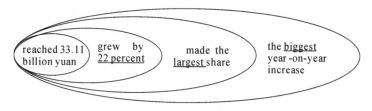

图 6-5 增强型态度韵律

图 6-5 中共有 4 处鉴赏资源,均为积极显性评价词汇,报道中国西南部云南省与"一带一路"沿线国家贸易往来密切,对外贸易额提升,通过发展对外贸易,有效推动中国与东盟以及拉美国家经济的发展,为"一带一路"建设提供良好的外部环境和发展动力。这 4 处鉴赏资源所表达的评价态度逐渐递增,构成增强型韵律模式,首先点明对外贸易额,然后根据海关数据指出同比增长的比例,接着连续用形容词最高级表明贸易额的激增,并给予该新闻事件最重要的社会评价。通过增强型态度韵律,新闻作者以时间顺序,通过客观数据,展现中国与"一带一路"沿线国家对外贸易的发展,评价强度不断提高,最终上升为最高价值评价,犹如音律由弱到强,像波浪般在语篇中层层递进,将评价态度推向高潮。这充分体现了新闻报道有理有据,逻辑缜密,促使读者理解并接受语篇立场,逻辑说服的修辞策略由此得以实现。

首先,本章借助 White 的新闻语类结构模型,统计并分析了"一带一路"对外新闻的态度资源在语篇中的分布规律，揭示了态度资源的三个子系统在各语步的分布情况。其次，运用评价理论态度系统和古典修辞理论，描述了态度资源在小句层面上如何构建渗透型、主导型和增强型韵律模式，实现情感说服、人品说服和逻辑说服的修辞策略。上述定量分析为下一章（第七章）的定性分析奠定了基础。

第七章 "一带一路"对外新闻
态度策略定性分析

　　第六章分析了态度资源在"一带一路"新闻语篇中的分布结构以及态度修辞策略的实现方式。本章采用定性分析的方法,从研究语料中选取"一带一路"分别在欧洲、亚洲、非洲和拉美地区发展的新闻报道进行实例分析,阐明语篇的语域要素以及新闻作者如何运用态度韵律策略实现修辞说服目的。

　　作为一种新型跨区域合作架构,"一带一路"倡议具有开放、包容、互利、共赢的特点。它不是中国单独推进或强加于他国的方案,也不是一个封闭性和排他性的方案,而是中国与欧亚非以及拉美各国共商、共营、共建、共享的开放的合作方案。当前,"一带一路"倡议主要包括欧洲、亚洲、非洲和拉美各个国家。由于对外新闻报道的侧重点不同,中国在与不同国家的对外关系上采取不同的举措,新闻作者也会根据不同的语域特征而采取相应的评价姿态和说服方式。

一、中欧新闻语篇的态度策略

欧洲大陆是"一带一路"倡议部署的主战场之一,而欧洲既是"中国梦"进程的竞争者也是合作者,因而中欧在"一带一路"倡议发展上有着千丝万缕的联系,欧洲自然而然也就成为中国"一带一路"外交宣传的重要目标。此外,欧洲作为西方政治舞台以及舆论场的中心之一,对"一带一路"倡议在世界范围内的形象构建有着重要影响。

作为横跨亚欧大陆的国家,俄罗斯在 1996 年与中国建立战略伙伴关系,20 多年来,两国在各个领域的合作都得到了极大的发展。2015 年 5 月,中俄两国元首共同签署了《中华人民共和国与俄罗斯联邦关于丝绸之路经济带建设和欧亚经济联盟建设对接合作的联合声明》,标志着两国对共建"一带一路"达成共识,这一战略性突破必将加快推进两国区域发展和区域经济一体化进程。

俄罗斯积极参加"一带一路"建设,这既是对该倡议既有成就的充分肯定,也必将为"一带一路"建设的继续推进注入新动能。俄罗斯地缘和经济优势使其成为共建"一带一路"的重要组成部分,而过去几年俄罗斯对与中国加强经贸合作的高度重视以及对"一带一路"倡议认识的不断提升也使得两国未来在"一带一路"框架下的合作大有可为。随着"一带一路"倡议正式成为两国合作的新平台,中俄合作将迈入全方位、高质量发展的新阶段,也有望对中欧整体合作形成积极的示范效应。下面以 2018 年 9 月 12 日发表于 Xinhua News Agency 上题为"Xi, Putin vow to promote ties regardless of global changes"的新闻为例,分析对外新闻的语域要素,按照态度韵律结构,阐明新闻作者如何运用态度韵律体现修辞策略。新闻原文如下:

Xi, Putin vow to promote ties regardless of global changes

Chinese President Xi Jinping and his Russian counterpart, Vladimir Putin, expressed their firm determination to promote bilateral ties and safeguard world peace and stability during their talks here on Tuesday.

Xi arrived in the Russian port city of Vladivostok earlier in the day for the fourth Eastern Economic Forum(EEF) at the invitation of Putin.

During their talks, Xi and Putin acknowledged that China-Russia ties have been developing with stronger momentum this year and have entered a new period of faster development on a higher level.

Regardless of the changes in the international situation, China and Russia will unswervingly promote their ties and steadfastly safeguard world peace and stability, said the two heads of state.

Recalling their productive meetings in Beijing and Johannesburg this year, Xi told Putin that the close high-level contacts between China and Russia have demonstrated the height and uniqueness of the bilateral relationship and showed that the two countries give top priority to the ties on their diplomatic agendas respectively.

Thanks to joint efforts of both sides, the political advantages of China-Russia relations have been translated into tangible cooperation fruits continuously, Xi said.

China and Russia have steadfastly supported each other in pursuing development paths that suit their respective national conditions and in safeguarding their security and development rights, setting an example of major-country relations and neighborhood interaction, Xi said.

He urged both sides to consolidate their traditional friendship, strengthen comprehensive coordination and promote the China-Russia comprehensive strategic partnership of coordination to a new height so as to better serve the interests of both peoples.

China and Russia should strengthen the synergy of the Belt and Road Initiative and the Eurasian Economic Union (EEU), expand cooperation in such fields as energy, agriculture, scientific and technological innovation and finance, promote steady implementation of major projects and boost joint research and development of cutting-edge science and technology, Xi said.

Since this year and the next year are designated as the years of local cooperation and exchange between China and Russia, the two countries should seize the opportunity to encourage more local participation in bilateral cooperation, Xi said.

Supporting each other in holding large-scale events has been a good tradition for China and Russia, Xi said.

The EEF, proposed by Putin, has become an important platform for pooling wisdom and jointly discussing regional cooperation, said the Chinese president, adding that he believes this year's forum will bring new opportunities for China and Russia to deepen regional cooperation, including Far East cooperation.

Both as permanent members of the United Nations (UN) Security Council and major emerging economies, China and Russia shoulder the task of safeguarding world peace and stability and promoting development and prosperity, Xi said.

He urged the two countries to maintain close communication and coordination within multilateral frameworks such as the UN, the Shanghai Cooperation Organization and BRICS, push forward political settlement of hotspot issues together with the international community, and jointly protect international equity and justice, as well as world peace and stability.

He also called on the two sides to firmly uphold the purposes and principles of the UN Charter, jointly oppose unilateralism and trade protectionism, and forge ahead with the construction of a new type of international relations and a community with a shared future for mankind.

Putin, for his part, expressed heart-felt gratitude and warm welcome for Xi's attendance at the EEF.

President Xi and I have kept close exchanges, which shows the high level of Russia-China ties, Putin said.

Hailing the robust momentum of the development of bilateral ties in recent years, Putin said the mutual trust between China and Russia has grown increasingly strong and bilateral cooperation in various fields such as politics, economy and security has been fruitful.

He said both sides should continue to promote the synergy of the EEU and the Belt and Road Initiative, expand cooperation in such fields as investment, energy, aerospace, finance and e-commerce, boost cultural and people-to-people exchanges and promote local cooperation.

Russia and China share many similar views on the current international situation，Putin said，calling on the two countries to enhance coordination and cooperation in international affairs，firmly oppose unilateralism，safeguard a fair and rational international order and realize common development and prosperity.

The two leaders also exchanged in-depth views on international and regional issues of common concern and witnessed the inking of multiple bilateral cooperation documents.

程微(2010)认为,态度韵律结构包含三个层次:态度韵律单位、态度韵律相和态度韵律阶段。语域要素包括语场、语式和语旨。该新闻的语场是习近平在第四届东方经济论坛上会见俄罗斯总统普京时达成的共识,即发展和深化中俄双边关系,加强合作,推动"一带一路"建设与欧亚经济联盟对接,实现中欧共同繁荣。语式是书面、正式的官方报道。语旨是新闻网站和读者,Xinhua News Agency 被称为"中国最有影响力的网站",读者是海内外想了解该倡议的各界人士,因此语篇内容单向流动,新闻网站是信息输出方,读者是接收方。

(一)态度韵律单位

态度韵律单位是指词汇层面的单个态度评价资源,涵盖情感、判断和鉴赏三个子系统,评价模式为显性或隐性,评价极性为积极或消极。

该新闻语篇各语步展开顺序为:开篇——详述——解释——详述——评论——背景。开篇语步包含标题和导语,新闻作者首先用显性判断资源(vow to promote ties)指出中俄两国领导人承诺,无论全球如何变化,也会促进两国之间的发展。接着继续用显性判断资源(expressed their firm determination;safeguard world peace and stability)揭示中俄两国的坚定立场,即促进双边关系,维护世界和平与稳定。开篇中两次积极判断资源都描述中俄两国相互合作、互为支持,共同维护两国的良好关系和世界安全。中俄作为"一带一路"沿线的重要大国,两国一直致力于睦邻友好的国际关系,通过加强彼此间的联系与合作,必将产生巨大的示范和带动效应,引导更多的国家加入"一带一路"倡议,这充分证明该倡议提出的正确性。

详述语步中,作者引述习近平话语,用判断资源描述中俄应维护好两国发展关系,加强"一带一路"倡议与欧亚经济联盟的协同作用,扩大合作领域,把中俄全面战略协作伙伴关系推向新的高度,才能更好地为两国人民的利益服务,表现了习近平主席的远见和卓识,为随后语篇的发展奠定了坚定积极的语调。

解释语步以鉴赏资源为主(a good tradition for China and Russia;an important platform for pooling wisdom;

bring new opportunities），指明中俄的交流与合作符合历史发展的必然趋势和时代潮流，也为其他国家和地区的发展带来新的机遇。评论语步通过情感资源（heart-felt gratitude and warm welcome），表达普京总统对两国高层的往来最真实的情感，也体现了中俄关系的高度发展。

最后，背景语步通过鉴赏资源（the robust momentum of the development of bilateral ties），表明两国关系发展的前景：继续推动欧亚经济联盟与"一带一路"倡议的对接，加强人文交流，促进地方合作。可见，该语篇的态度韵律单位发展模式是：以判断资源开篇，用鉴赏资源和情感资源展开报道，最后以鉴赏资源收尾。

（二）态度韵律相

态度韵律相是指在小句层面，由一组韵律单位构成，针对同一对象的评价资源群。该新闻开篇语步用两处显性判断资源构成一个态度韵律相，其评价对象是中俄两国领导人在促进双边关系，维护世界和平与稳定方面的能力。详述语步继续用判断资源构建态度韵律相，评价习近平主席作为国家领导人所具有的高超政治智慧和才能。解释语步通过鉴赏资源形成韵律相，评价中俄两国的往来与发展对不同区域乃至整个世界产生的影响和价值。评论语步中，由情感资源构成的态度韵律相突显俄罗斯政府对中国领导人参与双方的经济建设表示高兴和满意，也对中俄之间的进一步发展充满信心。背景语步通过鉴赏态度资源群形成评价两国未来发展的韵律相,阐明两国之间往来的价值和意义。可见,该语篇的态度韵律相推进模式为:开篇描绘中俄共同维护发展关系,顺应时代发展趋势,进而表现习主席优秀的判断力和决策力,然后表达中俄合作的深远意义以及俄罗斯方对习主席参加此次经济论坛的真实情感,最后阐述中俄近年来的发展历程和未来的发展形势。

(三)态度韵律阶段

态度韵律阶段是指在语篇层面,各语步的态度韵律发展模式。

该新闻开篇语步采用主导型韵律模式,报道中俄两国领导人共同承诺,要加强两国之间的合作,维护全球安全。该韵律模式以习主席和普京总统所表达的坚定信念为开场,奠定评价语调,随后多处判断资源与之产生呼应,衬托出中俄领导人应对全球变化时的从容不迫。

详述语步仍采用主导型韵律模式,以习近平主席优秀的领导力和非凡的才能为评价核心,从促进两国高层交往,维护双方权利以及加强"一带一路"倡议与欧亚经济联盟之间的协同作用等方面与之响应,展现习主席对中俄双方合作与发展的深刻理解。

解释语步通过增强型韵律模式,阐明中俄之间合作交流的历史意义和深远影响,鉴赏资源的评价对象不断扩大,评价强度逐步提升,从中俄发展,到世界未来,从中俄国家利益,到世界发展繁荣,从各国的合作交流,到国际社会的共同参与,韵律音量持续上升,彰显中俄合作的多重意义,从两国经济发展,到各国的参与协作,以及世界和平昌盛。可见,中俄两国关系发展的意义和重要性已关系到全球的和平与稳定,符合时代发展的趋势。评论语步采用渗透型韵律模式,报道普京总统对习主席出席此次论坛的感谢,对两国关系的发展持乐观态度,新闻人物的态度通过情感资源散布于每个小句,渗透在评论语步中,体现了中俄关系的高度发展,为世界和平发展营造和谐的氛围。

背景语步沿用增强型韵律模式,表明中俄两国关系的发展趋势以及未来发展前景,鉴赏评价强度逐渐上升,从扩大合作领域,实现战略对接,到构建国际新秩序,再到实现全人类共同发展与繁荣,韵律音阶不断提升。

因此,该语篇的态度韵律阶段进展模式为:以主导型韵律模式开篇,多处判断资源响应开场音符,形成回音和共鸣;然后用增强型和渗透型模式推进报道,一连串鉴赏资源和情感资源不断推高韵律音阶;最后借助鉴赏资源,在增强型韵律模式中收尾,态度韵律弥漫于整个语篇当中。

(四) 态度修辞策略

该语篇首先通过判断资源,形成主导型态度韵律,表明中俄两国领导人在推动建设新型国际关系方面所具备的能力,以及习近平主席优秀的判断力和决策力,取得读者的信任,体现人品说服的修辞策略;然后运用鉴赏资源,构建增强型态度韵律,基于客观事实,通过逻辑推理,逐级提升评价强度,深刻地阐释中俄合作的重要性和现实意义,让读者深信不疑,实现逻辑说服的修辞策略;最后通过情感资源,形成渗透型态度韵律,展现普京总统对习主席参加此次会谈的情感反应,烘托出积极乐观的评价立场,读者身处其中,自然体会其用意,接受语篇立场,体现情感说服的修辞策略。综观全文,中欧"一带一路"对外新闻更注重人品说服的修辞策略,较大篇幅运用判断资源和主导型韵律模式报道中国和欧洲各国领导人的外交言论,体现他们高瞻远瞩的政治觉悟和一心为民的治国理念。

二、中亚新闻语篇的态度策略

中国提出"一带一路"倡议,旨在同其他沿线国家实现协同发展、互利共赢、共同繁荣的愿望。以"一带一路"亚洲国家为背景,是考虑到沿线亚洲国家具有较强的战略地位和优越的地理条件,并且大部分都属于发展中国家,这与中国当前经济发展水平相似。当前,在全球经济一体化进程中,区域经济一体化的重要性越来越明显,各国都在积极开展区域性经济合作。随着"一带一路"建设的不断推进,中国与"一带一路"沿线国家之间的贸易投资关系也在不断加强。而沿线亚洲国家作为"一带一路"倡议实施的出发点,起到了承前启后的作用。中国与沿线亚洲国家的贸易发展直接影响到"一带一路"倡议的成功实施。

中亚地区是"丝绸之路经济带"的第一站,它在"一带一路"的向西延展中扮演着一个整体性的角色。习近平主席访问中亚国家时提出的共建"丝绸之路经济带"的倡议,就考虑到该地区重要的位置及其巨大的发展潜力。

乌兹别克斯坦位于中亚的中心位置,是中亚第二大经济体,在中亚地区具有重要的战略地位,是丝绸之路经济带建设不可或缺的重要参与方。中国和乌兹别克斯坦传统友谊源远流长,中乌两国建交以来,一直保持着健康稳定的合作关系,国家高层交往密切,政治互信不断增强,安全合作卓有成效,经济合作成果丰硕,人文交流日益密切。特别是习近平主席提出建设"丝绸之路经济带"的倡议后,立即得到了乌兹别克斯坦前总统卡里莫夫和乌国社会各界的支持。2014 年 5 月 20 日,国家主席习近平在上海会见乌兹别克斯坦前总统卡里莫夫时,乌总统表示,乌方愿积极参与建设丝绸之路经济带,做中国坚定的合作伙伴,促进经贸往来和互联互通,把乌兹别克斯坦的发展同中国的繁荣更紧密联系在一起。近年来,伴随"一带一路"倡议稳步推进,中乌各领域互利合作不断扩大,双边经贸合作不断迈上新台阶。下面以 2017 年 5 月 13 日发表于 Xinhua News Agency 上题为 "Xi urges broader cooperation with Uzbekistan in building B & R" 的新闻为例,分析对外新闻的语域要素,按照态度韵律结构,阐明新闻作者如何运用态度韵律体现修辞策略。新闻原文如下:

Xi urges broader cooperation with Uzbekistan in building B&R

Chinese President Xi Jinping called for expanding cooperation with Uzbekistan to achieve new progress in carrying out the Belt and Road Initiative on May 12, 2017.

Xi made the remarks when meeting with his Uzbek counterpart Shavkat Mirziyoyev, who is in Beijing to attend the Belt and Road Forum for International Cooperation.

Xi said that over the 25 years since the two countries established diplomatic relations, bilateral ties have achieved "leapfrog development" and the two countries have forged a comprehensive strategic partnership with sincerity, mutual trust, mutual benefits and win-win cooperation.

The two countries have cooperated closely under the Belt and Road framework and implemented a series of major projects, delivering tangible benefits to the people of both countries, Xi said.

He called for continued mutual support on issues concerning each other's core interests and major concerns, consolidating and deepening political and strategic mutual trust for common development and prosperity.

Xi said China is willing to maintain close communication and coordination with Uzbekistan on issues including international affairs, situation in Central Asia and development of the Shanghai Cooperation Organization.

He urged the two countries to dovetail their development strategies, outline priorities for cooperation, explore potential to enhance economic and trade cooperation, boost bilateral trade, optimize trade structure, and ensure the long-term and stable growth of bilateral trade.

China would also like to expand cooperation with Uzbekistan on industrial capacity, investment as well as the building of industrial zones and infrastructure based on equality, voluntariness, mutual benefits and win-win cooperation, he said.

Calling China a great neighbor of Uzbekistan, Mirziyoyev said Uzbekistan appreciates China's support for the country in taking a development path in line with its national conditions.

He said China's role in promoting world peace, stability and development is crucial.

He noted Uzbekistan will continue adhering to the one-China policy and support China's efforts in combating the "three evil forces" of terrorism, separatism and extremism.

Mirziyoyev also called for deepening cooperation with

China in areas including economy and trade, investment, industrial capacity, infrastructure and water conservation.

After the meeting, the two leaders signed a joint declaration to deepen the comprehensive strategic partnership.

The two countries will continue to support each other on issues of core interests including national sovereignty, security and territorial integrity, according to the declaration.

Neither side will allow a third country, any organization or group to commit activities on its soil that will damage the other side's national sovereignty, security and territorial integrity.

In the joint declaration, the two sides agreed on the necessity of constructing an efficient and convenient railway passage between China and Uzbekistan, and they will step up coordination on the China-Kyrgyzstan-Uzbekistan railway project.

该新闻的语场是习近平主席与乌兹别克斯坦领导人在"一带一路"国际合作论坛会议上强调要加强双方合作,共同推动"一带一路"建设。语式是书面、正式的官方报道。该语场是肯定了"一带一路"倡议对乌国的积极影响。语旨是新闻网站和读者,因此语篇内容单向流动,新闻网站是信息输出方,读者是接收方。

（一）态度韵律单位

该语篇各语步展开顺序为:开篇——详述——解释——背景——评论。

开篇语步包括标题和导语,新闻作者首先在标题部分用显性判断资源指出中国强调在"一带一路"建设方面与乌国展开更广泛的合作。在导语中,作者继续用判断资源(called for expanding cooperation with Uzbekistan)强调习近平呼吁与乌方扩大合作,最后用积极判断资源(achieve new progress)表明中乌双方共同推动"一带一路"建设取得新进展。开篇中3次积极判断资源都转述自习近平,表现习近平主席卓越的政治才能,积极加强与"一带一路"沿线国家的合作,推动该倡议的健康发展,也为随后语篇的展开奠定了坚定积极的语调。

详述语步中,作者引述习近平话语,用判断资源(have forged a comprehensive strategic partnership;implemented a series of major projects)描述中乌两国自建交以来所取得的历史成就,以及两国在"一带一路"倡议下实施的一系列重大项目,树立中国亲邻友好的国际形象。

解释语步以鉴赏资源为主(common development and prosperity;close communication and coordination),阐明中乌合作的重要性和意义就是保持亲密交流与合作,实现共同发展繁荣,体现了"一带一路"倡议背景下,合作共赢才是发展的主流。背景语步仍通过鉴赏资源（China's role in promoting world peace, stability and development is crucial），介绍中国在维护世界和平与发展等方面的作用至关重要，即深化双方的合作领域，坚持走符合国情的发展道路。

最后评论语步通过情感资源点评中乌两国合作的发展前景（The two countries will continue to support each other），指明相互支持，合作共赢是两国发展的途径和目标。可见，该语篇的态度韵律单位发展模式为：以判断资源开篇，用鉴赏资源展开报道，最后以情感资源收尾。

（二）态度韵律相

该新闻开篇语步用 3 处判断资源构成一个态度韵律相，其评价对象是习近平主席的才能。详述语步继续用判断资源群构建成 1 个评价中乌两国合作能力的韵律相。解释语步和背景语步都通过鉴赏资源群形成评价中乌双方合作领域和内容的韵律相，表现该合作的价值。评论语步中，由情感资源构成的态度韵律相突显中乌领导人对双方的合作表示满意，也对两国的未来发展寄予厚望。可见，该语篇的态度韵律相推进模式为：开篇描绘习主席的卓越才能，进而表现中国政府的能力与可靠性，然后阐述中乌合作的领域和内容，突显历史重要性和现实意义，最后传达两国领导人对未来发展的真实态度，展现该合作的发展目标。

（三）态度韵律阶段

该新闻开篇语步采用主导型韵律模式，报道习近平主席呼吁扩大与乌兹别克斯坦的合作,推动"一带一路"建设取得新进展。该韵律模式以习主席在"一带一路"国际合作高峰论坛上发表的言论为开场音符,奠定评价基调,随后多处判断资源与之产生共鸣,衬托习近平作为国家领导人所具有的高超领导力和感召力。

详述语步仍采用主导型韵律模式,以中乌两国真诚互信、互利共赢的全面战略伙伴关系为评价核心,从两国发展、密切合作等方面与之响应,回声不断,展现中乌两国政府对"一带一路"建设的深刻理解和坚定信念。

解释语步通过增强型韵律模式,阐明双方合作与实现共同发展的辩证关系,鉴赏资源的评价对象不断扩大,评价强度逐步上升,从两国相互支持,到扩大合作领域,从两国共同繁荣,到世界未来发展,表明两国合作的多重意义。可见,中乌合作虽是在两国之间进行的,但其本质和影响力已经超越国界,关系到不同地区乃至全世界的发展。

背景语步沿用增强型韵律模式,表明中乌两国共谋发展,相互支持,鉴赏评价强度逐渐升高,从深化战略合作,到国家核心利益上相互支持,再到维护世界的和平与稳定,韵律音阶不断上升。

评论语步采用渗透型韵律模式,报道中乌两国领导人支持双方的发展道路和相关政策,对两国未来的合作前景充满期待。新闻人物的态度通过情感资源散布于每个小句,渗透在评论语步中,表明"一带一路"倡议下,中乌合作符合两国人民的根本利益,也为该倡议的推行奠定了良好的民意基础。

因此,该语篇的态度韵律阶段进展模式为:以主导型韵律模式开篇,多处判断资源响应开场音符,形成回音和共鸣;然后用增强型韵律模式推进报道,一连串鉴赏资源不断提高韵律音阶;最后在渗透型韵律模式中收尾,借助情感资源,态度韵律弥漫于语篇结尾。

(四)态度修辞策略

该新闻语篇首先通过判断资源,形成主导型态度韵律,表明习主席的真知灼见,塑造了中国领导人致力于促进"一带一路"沿线国家共同进步和富裕的积极形象,博取读者信任,体现了人品说服的修辞策略;然后运用鉴赏资源,构建增强型态度韵律,分析具体事实,逐渐扩大评价对象,让读者深刻地认识到中乌合作的必要性和重大意义,实现逻辑说服的修辞策略。最后通过情感资源,形成渗透型态度韵律,展现中乌两国在深化合作方面的情感反应,营造出积极乐观、和谐融洽的评价立场,令读者不禁感同身受,促使其接受语篇立场,实现情感说服策略。综观全文,中亚"一带一路"对外新闻更注重逻辑说服的修辞策略,较大篇幅运用鉴赏资源和增强型韵律模式报道中国和亚洲各国的合作领域、方式和层次,体现区域合作的巨大潜力和重大意义。

三、中非新闻语篇的态度策略

中非关系发展的历史由来已久，中国自古以来就与非洲国家和地区有着良好的经济与文化交流。单就海上丝绸之路而言，公元 14 世纪郑和在下西洋的过程中就到访过非洲中东部海岸的部分国家和地区，构建了与非洲航线沿途国家和地区良好的贸易关系，从此中非贸易关系打开了发展大门。这不仅为之后的中非"丝路贸易"构建友谊桥梁，也为非洲作为当代中国"一带一路"倡议中的重要合作对象奠定了良好的历史基础。

自新中国成立以来，中国对非关系在平等互利、合作共赢、开放包容、共同发展等原则的指引下，实现从"新型战略伙伴关系"到"全面战略合作伙伴关系"的演变。2013 年"一带一路"倡议提出后，中非关系进入了全新的发展阶段。"一带一路"倡议为中非间的贸易发展、投资合作、基础设施建设和产能合作提供了新的平台。可以说，中非合作与"一带一路"倡议是相辅相成的关系，中非双方相互需要并互为机遇。此后非洲国家积极参与并推进"一带一路"建设。在 2018 年9 月举行的中非合作论坛北京峰会上，习近平主席表示非洲是"一带一路"的历史和自然延伸，是重要参与方，中非双方一致同意将"一带一路"同联合国《2030 年可持续发展议程》、非盟《2063 年议程》和非洲各国发展战略紧密对接，加强"五通"建设,促进双方"一带一路"产能合作。总体而言,"一带一路"倡议推动中非合作的升级,不仅有利于非洲一体化和工业化进程,有助于中非领域合作的全方位深入,还为中非合作向更高维度、更深层次发展创造了机遇。下面以 2018 年 9 月 4 日发表于 Xinhua News Agency 上题为 "China supports Africa jointly building Belt and Road: Xi"的新闻为例,分析对外新闻的语域要素,按照态度韵律结构,阐明新闻作者如何运用态度韵律体现修辞策略。新闻原文如下:

China supports Africa jointly building Belt and Road: Xi

China supports African countries in jointly building the Belt and Road to share the win-win outcomes, said President Xi Jinping Monday when addressing the High-Level Dialogue Between Chinese and African Leaders and Business Representatives.

China stands ready to strengthen comprehensive cooperation with African countries to build a road of high-quality development that is suited to national conditions, inclusive and beneficial to all, Xi said in his keynote speech at the meeting, also the Sixth Conference of Chinese and African Entrepreneurs.

Realizing common prosperity for the people of all nations, including African people, is an important part of building a community with a shared future for humanity, Xi said in his speech themed "walk together towards prosperity."

"Africa is an extension of the Belt and Road development historically and naturally and an important participant in the initiative," Xi said.

China does not attach any political strings to its investment in Africa under the Belt and Road Initiative, nor does it interfere in African countries' internal affairs or impose its demands on others, Xi noted.

The China-Africa cooperation under the initiative targets inadequate infrastructure and other key constraints on Africa's development, "with funds to be used where they count most," Xi said.

He said China and Africa's joint development of the Belt and Road completely follows established international rules, and China is ready to strengthen third-party cooperation with any country that has the capability and the intent.

China encourages and supports two-way investment, does not pursue trade surplus and is willing to create conditions for expanding import, Xi said.

China welcomes entrepreneurs worldwide, including

those from Africa, to invest and develop in China and encourages Chinese entrepreneurs to explore and develop business in Africa, so as to jointly promote the Belt and Road, Xi said.

He asked Chinese and African entrepreneurs to grow together with the people of China and Africa, jointly making great achievements.

Xi also urged entrepreneurs to seize this historic opportunity for innovation, learn from each other and create new ways to cooperate.

Entrepreneurs should also shoulder social responsibility, respect local cultural customs and serve as a bridge for China-Africa friendship in the process of economic cooperation, Xi said.

"China is willing to work hard side by side with our African brothers to share the fruits of development and together set foot on a path of happiness where people live a better life," Xi said.

African leaders also delivered speeches at the meeting, including South African President Cyril Ramaphosa, Chadian President Idriss Deby Itno, Djiboutian President Ismail Omar Guelleh, Mauritanian President Mohamed Ould Abdel Aziz, Namibian President Hage Geingob and Nigerian

President Muhammadu Buhari.

Noting that the ten cooperation plans announced at the 2015 Johannesburg summit of the FOCAC have given a strong impetus to comprehensive economic and social development in Africa, these leaders said the Belt and Road Initiative aligns with the economic development projects of African countries.

The African leaders also expect deep engagement in Belt and Road development via the Beijing summit and to work with China to build an even stronger China-Africa community with a shared future.

Representatives of both Chinese and African businesses expressed their willingness to actively participate in the Belt and Road cooperation and contribute to the building of a China-Africa community with a shared future.

该新闻的语场是习近平在中非领导人和企业代表高层对话上表示,中国与非洲国家加强合作,共建"一带一路",构建中非命运共同体,实现互利共赢。语式是书面、正式的官方报道。语旨是新闻网站和读者,因此语篇内容单向流动,新闻网站是信息输出方,读者是接收方。

(一)态度韵律单位

该新闻语篇各语步展开顺序为:开篇——详述——解

释——背景——评论。

开篇语步包含标题和导语,新闻作者首先转述习近平话语,用情感资源(support)和判断资源(jointly building Belt and Road)表示中国支持非洲国家加入"一带一路"建设,在导语中沿用相同的转述策略,用判断资源(to share the win-win outcomes)指出中国愿与非洲国家共享"一带一路"建设的成果,实现互利共赢。虽然开篇中的评价资源表面上修饰"一带一路"倡议,但更重要的是,它表现了中国政府积极推动非洲国家发展的坚定信念,也展现了习近平主席不忘初心,始终秉承"一带一路"建设的原则和理念,为随后中非合作的展开提供了坚实的基础和广阔的空间。可见,该处的评价资源仍为隐性判断资源。

详述语步中,作者继续引述习近平话语,用判断资源(China stands ready to strengthen comprehensive cooperation with African countries)描述中国愿同非洲国家加强全面合作,实现非洲人民乃至各国人民的共同繁荣,构建人类命运共同体,这充分展现了中国作为负责任大国的国际形象。解释语步以鉴赏资源(an important participant in the initiative)为主,阐明非洲与中国"一带一路"建设的渊源,中国不附加任何政治条件为非洲国家的发展提供基础设施建设和资金支持,体现该倡议的透明性和公正性。

背景语步通过鉴赏资源(a strong impetus to comprehensive economic and social development in Africa),

表明"一带一路"倡议符合非洲国家经济发展,中非双方愿积极参与"一带一路"合作,为构建中非命运共同体做出贡献。

评论语步通过情感资源点评"一带一路"产生的积极影响(The African leaders also expect deep engagement in Belt and Road development):非洲国家期待深入参与"一带一路"建设,构建中非命运共同体。可见,该语篇的态度韵律单位发展模式是:以判断资源开篇,用鉴赏资源展开报道,最后以情感资源收尾。

(二)态度韵律相

该新闻开篇语步用 3 处判断资源构成 1 个态度韵律相,描述习近平主席的主张和愿景,其评价对象是习主席的才能。详述语步继续用判断资源群构成 1 个评价中国能力的韵律相。解释语步通过鉴赏资源群评价"一带一路"建设的宗旨和原则,表现该倡议的构成和价值。背景语步仍通过鉴赏资源群点评该倡议的价值和深远影响。最后,评论语步中,由情感资源构成的韵律相突出非洲国家对"一带一路"倡议的信心。可见,该语篇的态度韵律相推进模式为:开篇描写习主席致力于帮助非洲国家实现互利共赢的个人形象,进而表现出中国政府在实现共同繁荣这一目标方面所具备的能力,然后阐述"一带一路"倡议的内涵,传达中国对中非双向合作的积极态度,最后转述中非参会代表对加入"一带一路"建设的强烈愿望,点明"一带一路"倡议符合中非的发展,展现该倡议的发展前景。

（三）态度韵律阶段

该新闻开篇语步采用主导型韵律模式,报道中国和非洲国家共同参与"一带一路"建设,共享发展成果。该韵律模式以习近平在大会上的宣言为开场音符,奠定评价基调,随后多处判断资源与之产生共鸣,烘托出习近平对"一带一路"建设的坚定信念和深刻理解。

详述语步仍采用主导型韵律模式,以中国敢于担当的大国形象和实现人类共同繁荣的目标为评价核心,从加强全面合作、实现共同繁荣和构建人类命运共同体等方面与之响应,回声不断,展现了中国与非洲国家同舟共济、共同发展的大国形象。

解释语步通过增强型韵律模式,阐明"一带一路"倡议和非洲各国发展的辩证关系,鉴赏资源的评价对象不断扩大,评价强度逐步上升,从中国的"一带一路"建设,到非洲国家的共同参与,从非洲国家的利益,到全球各国共同发展,从中非的合作共赢,到与世界各国共享繁荣,韵律音量持续调高,突显"一带一路"建设的跨国界、跨大陆、跨民族的多重意义。可见,该倡议为中非的经济和文化发展以及世界其他国家的合作往来提供广阔的平台和发展空间。背景语步沿用增强型韵律模式,表明"一带一路"倡议逐渐深入人心,获得非洲国家的广泛接受,鉴赏评价强度不断升高,从推动非洲经济社会发展,到契合非洲国家经济发展项目,韵律音阶不断上行。

评论语步采用渗透型韵律模式,报道非洲领导人和中非企业代表支持"一带一路"倡议,对该倡议的发展充满期待和信心。新闻人物的态度通过情感资源散布于每个小句,渗透在评论语步中,表明习近平主席对"一带一路"倡议的阐述赢得与会者的一致赞赏,为中非的发展营造积极乐观的氛围。

因此,该语篇的态度韵律阶段进展模式为:以主导型韵律模式开篇,多处判断资源响应开场音符,形成回音和共鸣;然后用增强型韵律模式推进报道,一连串鉴赏资源不断提高韵律音阶;最后在渗透型韵律模式中收尾,借助情感资源,态度韵律弥漫于语篇结尾。

(四)态度修辞策略

该新闻语篇首先通过判断资源,形成主导型态度韵律,表现习近平主席胸怀天下的个人形象,积极推动与非洲国家的交流合作,取得读者信任,体现人品说服的修辞策略;然后运用鉴赏资源,构建增强型态度韵律,以客观事实为依据,通过逐步分析,评价范围不断扩大,令人信服地阐述"一带一路"倡议是实现人类共同繁荣进步的重要保障;最后通过情感资源,形成渗透型态度韵律,展现中非领导人和其他参会者的情感反应,塑造出积极向上、信心满满的评价立场,读者身处其中,容易"感情用事",接受语篇立场,体现情感说服的修辞策略。综观全篇,中非"一带一路"对外新闻更注重情感说服的修辞策略,较大篇幅运用情感资源和渗透型韵律模式报道非洲各国加入"一带一路"建设的强烈愿望,以及对该倡议的赞赏和信任,强调该倡议在非洲大陆的历史文化背景,尤其是对非洲普通民众的意义,体现"一带一路"在非洲逐渐深入人心,建立了坚实的民意基础。

四、中拉新闻语篇的态度策略

"一带一路"倡议顺应世界多极化、经济全球化、文化多样化的潮流,秉持开放的区域合作精神,致力于维护全球自由贸易体系和开放型世界经济。共建"一带一路"符合国际社会的根本利益,彰显人类社会共同理想和美好追求,是国际合作以及全球治理新模式的积极探索,将为世界和平发展增添新的正能量。2017 年 5 月召开的"一带一路"高峰论坛得到拉美各国以及全世界的广泛参与,阿根廷和智利两国的总统也出席了这一峰会。其间,智利提出扩大"一带一路"倡议覆盖拉美及加勒比国家;阿根廷期待中企参与包括"两洋通道"在内的基础设施互联互通建设,并与中国在能源、教育、文化及农业等领域签署务实合作文件。这足以体现出"一带一路"的开放和包容特征与拉美国家所秉持的贸易开放政策的契合度。

"南南合作"是历史趋势,早在 16 世纪下半叶,中国与墨西哥之间就开辟出了一条"太平洋丝绸之路"。2014 年,习主席出访拉美时提出促进中拉经济合作的三大引擎和六大领域,推动中拉务实合作和产业对接全面发展。2016 年,习主席出访拉美三国并与厄瓜多尔和智利建立全面战略合作伙伴关系。可见,潜力巨大的拉美新兴市场属于国家"走出去"战略的目标市场,是"一带一路"的延伸和补充。

中厄建交 36 年来,双边政治经济关系发展顺畅,两国关系获得长足发展,政治互信不断增强,务实合作不断推进。在当前"一带一路"倡议及中拉关系日益密切的大背景下,中厄利用各自比较优势,结合各自发展战略,扩大贸易与投资力度,实现产业对接,深化战略合作,将中厄全面战略伙伴关系推向更高水平。下面以 2018 年 12 月 13 日发表于 *China Daily* 上题为 "Xi welcomes Ecuador to help build Belt & Road"的新闻为例,分析对外新闻的语域要素,按照态度韵律结构,阐明新闻作者如何运用态度韵律实现修辞功能。新闻原文如下:

Xi welcomes Ecuador to help build Belt & Road

China and Ecuador signed on Wednesday a cooperative document on jointly building the Belt and Road,drawing the two countries into a closer relationship.

The signing was witnessed by President Xi Jinping and his Ecuadorian counterpart, Lenin Moreno, during Moreno's three-day visit to China,which started on Tuesday.

More than 140 cooperative agreements on the joint construction of the Belt and Road have been signed between China and other countries or international organization.

During the meeting with Moreno, Xi said China welcomes Ecuador to participate in building the Belt and Road and jointly promote cooperation in such areas as industrial capacity, agriculture, information technology and new energy.

Ecuador is welcome in the Chinese market and to share the opportunities provided by China's development, Xi said. He said China never attaches any political strings to its financial cooperation with the Latin American country.

While the Chinese government asks Chinese enterprises to abide by local laws and regulations when doing business in Ecuador, it also hopes their legitimate rights and interests will be protected, Xi said.

He praised Moreno for his dedication to deepening the friendly cooperation between the two countries since he took office.

Promoting the healthy and stable development of bilateral ties is in line with the fundamental interests of both countries and their people, it also conforms to the trend of times, featuring peace, development, cooperation and win-win results, Xi said.

Xi called on both countries to have more frequent high-level exchanges, strengthen strategic coordination, share experience in governing a state, promote understanding and support for each other's development path, and firmly support each other on issues concerning core interests and major concerns.

China and Ecuador have the same or similar positions on major international and regional issues, Xi said, urging the two countries to jointly maintain multilateralism, promote the reform of the global governance system and safeguard the legitimate rights and interests of developing countries.

Moreno said the Belt and Road is an important international public contribution from China and connects the two countries in a closer manner.

Ecuador welcomes and thanks China's financial support as it bears significance for promoting the country's infrastructure construction, he said.

His country hopes to expand exports to China, host the China-Latin America business summit and make exchanges with China in the field of scientific and technological innovation, he added.

该新闻的语场是习近平与厄瓜多尔总统签署共建"一带一路"合作协议,加强各领域的合作,为两国的发展创造更好的前景。语式是在网站上以文字形式呈现的新闻语篇。语旨是新闻网站和读者,*China Daily* 是中国最优质的新闻平台之一,读者是海内外关注"一带一路"倡议的各界人士,因此语篇内容单向流动,新闻网站是信息输出方,读者是接收方。

(一)态度韵律单位

该新闻语篇各语步展开顺序为:开篇——详述——解释——背景——评论。

开篇语步包含标题和导语,新闻作者首先用显性情感资源和判断资源指出中国欢迎厄瓜多尔帮助"一带一路"建设,在导语中运用判断资源再次强调中厄两国共建"一带一路"(jointly building the Belt and Road),并用鉴赏资源表明该倡议的价值和意义(drawing the two countries into a closer relationship)。开篇中的积极态度资源都修饰"一带一路"倡议,可见,该倡议受到其他国家的肯定和认可。详述语步中,作者引述习近平的话语,并用判断资源(participate in building the Belt and Road and jointly promote cooperation)揭示习近平主席推崇睦邻友好的国际关系,积极推动拉美国家参与"一带一路"建设,努力实现中拉各国的共同发展,表现了习主席致力于维护世界和平、追求共同繁荣的领导风范。

解释语步以鉴赏资源为主(the healthy and stable development of bilateral ties; fundamental interests),阐述"一带一路"倡议下,中厄双方关系的良好发展符合两国的根本利益,顺应时代的潮流,体现该倡议对人类发展的深远影响。

背景语步仍通过鉴赏资源（the Belt and Road is an important international public contribution from China）介绍"一带一路"倡议对国际社会做出的重要贡献：中厄两国在此背景下，关系更加紧密，共同维护发展中国家利益。

最后评论语步通过情感资源指出厄瓜多尔对中方提供的支持表示欢迎和感谢（Ecuador welcomes and thanks China's financial support），两国相互合作，共同进步。可见，该语篇的态度韵律单位发展模式为：以判断资源开篇，用鉴赏资源展开报道，最后以情感资源收尾。

（二）态度韵律相

该新闻开篇语步用 2 处显性判断资源构成 1 个评价中国能力的韵律相。详述语步继续用判断资源群构成 1 个态度韵律相，其评价对象是习近平主席的能力。解释和背景语步通过鉴赏资源群形成评价"一带一路"倡议的韵律相，表现该倡议的构成和价值。评论语步中，由情感资源构成的韵律相表明中厄双方对彼此的合作、未来的发展以及"一带一路"的建设充满期待和信心。可见，该语篇的态度韵律相推进模式为：开篇描绘中国政府的能力，进而表现习近平主席的才能，然后阐述"一带一路"倡议的影响和意义，最后传递中厄对双方合作的真实感受。

（三）态度韵律阶段

该新闻语篇开篇采用主导型韵律模式，报道厄瓜多尔加入"一带一路"建设,与中国共建"一带一路"倡议。该韵律模式以习近平欢迎厄瓜多尔加入"一带一路"建设为开场,由此展开,随后多处判断资源与之相呼应,向读者呈现出中国政府致力于构建中拉合作关系,有能力开展具体务实的合作项目。

详述语步继续采用主导型韵律模式,以习主席高尚的品格,德才兼备的形象为评价核心,从促进合作、分享发展机遇和相互尊重、和平发展等方面与之相呼应,展现习主席良好的人文素养和道德情怀。

解释语步通过增强型韵律模式,指明两国关系的发展与构建人类命运共同体的辩证关系,鉴赏资源的评价对象不断扩大,评价强度逐渐上升,从两国发展,到世界未来,从两国人民利益,到人类繁荣进步,从两国交流发展,到全球合作共赢,韵律音量持续上升,彰显两国关系发展的深刻意义,从人民幸福生活,到两国经济发展,以及人类和平昌盛。背景语步沿用增强型韵律模式,表明"一带一路"倡议对国际社会做出的重大贡献,鉴赏评价强度逐渐升高,从促进两国关系发展,到维护发展中国家利益,再到推动全球治理体系改革。可见,该倡议虽是中国提出,但其意义和影响力已超越国界,是全人类共同事业。

评价语步采用渗透型韵律模式,报道"一带一路"倡议下,中厄两国相互支持与合作,对该倡议的发展充满期待,新闻作者的态度通过情感资源散布于每个小句,渗透在评论语步中,为"一带一路"的发展创造团结乐观的氛围。

因此,该语篇的态度韵律阶段发展模式为:主导型韵律模式开篇,多处判断资源响应开场音符,形成回音和共鸣;然后用增强型韵律模式推进报道,一连串鉴赏资源不断提高韵律音阶;最后以渗透型韵律模式收尾,借助情感资源,态度韵律弥漫于语篇结尾。

(四)态度修辞策略

该新闻语篇首先通过判断资源,形成主导型态度韵律,表现中国政府在"一带一路"建设方面的能力,以及习近平主席正直、勇于担当的个人形象,取得读者信任,体现人品说服的修辞策略;然后运用鉴赏资源,构建增强型态度韵律,根据具体事实,通过实例分析,逐步提高评价强度,深刻地阐释"一带一路"对于建设人类命运共同体的特殊意义,实现逻辑说服的修辞策略;最后通过情感资源,形成渗透型态度韵律,展现中厄两国对彼此合作的情感反应,营造出和谐、乐观的评价氛围,促使读者接受新闻作者观点,体现情感说服的修辞策略。综观全文,中拉"一带一路"对外新闻更注重逻辑说服的修辞策略,较大篇幅运用鉴赏资源和增强型韵律模式报道中国与拉美各国合作项目的潜力和意义,体现"一带一路"建设和拉美地区的发展需求高度契合。

本章结合评价理论态度系统和古典修辞理论,对"一带一路"对外新闻语篇中的态度资源进行定性分析,通过态度韵律结构,阐释了语篇中态度资源的修辞策略,发现新闻语篇可以通过判断资源,形成主导型态度韵律,实现人品说服的修辞策略;运用鉴赏资源,构建增强型态度韵律,体现逻辑说服的修辞策略;通过情感资源,形成渗透型态度韵律,表现情感说服的修辞策略。最终,新闻作者与读者对新闻事件达成一致的积极评价立场,推动"一带一路"倡议的对外传播,促进该倡议深入人心,为"一带一路"建设奠定民意基础。

第八章　结　论

一、研究主要发现

本研究运用评价理论的介入和态度系统，结合语类结构与修辞功能理论，分析中国"一带一路"对外新闻语篇，探究此类语篇中各部分的介入和态度策略分布规律、韵律话语模式和修辞话语策略。研究结果如下：

第一，新闻作者为了吸引读者兴趣，"一带一路"对外新闻语篇的开篇部分，往往运用单声策略呈现新闻标题，为了展现客观中立的报道风格，用承认策略推出新闻导语，话语空间由此打开。在详述部分，新闻作者充分运用承认策略，转述不同新闻参与者的话语，尽可能真实还原新闻事件，话语空间进一步扩展。在解释部分，新闻作者运用支持策略，压缩对话空间，支持转述对象，承担转述话语的人际责任，为读者揭开新闻事件各元素间的逻辑关系、前因后果，解除读者心中的迷惑。在评论部分，新闻作者继续运用支持策略压缩对话空间，力图聚焦转述观点，影响读者对新闻事件的价值判断和评价立场,拉拢读者与自己结成评价同盟。在背景部分,新闻作者通过单声策略描述类似事件、后续影响等,关闭对话空间,用公认事实对比眼前新闻,巩固与读者的态度同盟,引导读者接受新闻作者植入语篇的评价立场。

第二,对外新闻语篇往往用判断资源开篇和详述,用鉴赏资源进行解释和提供背景,最后用情感资源展开评论。"一带一路"对外新闻语篇的开篇语步主要对新闻人物的行为做出积极判断,是语篇核心人际意义的体现。详述语步是对开篇语步中的内容进行具体描述,所以两语步都是以判断资源为评价模式。鉴赏资源在对外新闻语篇中的分布主要集中在背景语步和解释语步。背景语步介绍新闻事件的发展过程,解释语步是展现新闻事件的前因后果,两语步旨在描述新闻事件的价值和构成以及新闻人物对该事件的反应。情感资源运用比例最高的是评论语步,该语步是对新闻事件的社会意义、情感影响等进行点评,旨在操纵读者的评价姿态。

第三,随着"一带一路"对外新闻语篇展开,各阶段介入策略为语篇构建的话语空间呈现出"关闭——扩展——收缩——关闭"的趋势,如此循环往复,形成伸缩有序的韵律话语模式。与此同时,态度韵律通常以主导型模式开场,奠定韵律基调,由多个评价音符形成回音,然后用增强型韵律模式,提升音阶,调高音量,最终用渗透型韵律模式,将评价态度融入语篇尾声。

第四,判断资源主要通过主导型态度韵律实现人品说服策略，鉴赏资源主要通过增强型态度韵律实现逻辑说服策略，情感资源主要通过渗透型态度韵律实现情感说服策略。判断是按照伦理、道德及法律对人的品行做出的评价。在对外新闻语篇中，新闻作者用表达判断意义的词汇构建主导型态度韵律来陈述其对某行为或人品的判断，表现新闻当事人的人品，赢得读者信任，"以德服人"，实现人品说服策略。鉴赏是对事件、事物和现象的评价。鉴赏资源通过增强型态度韵律体现新闻记者对新闻事件的反应以及对该事件的构成和价值做出评价，以引导读者去考量新闻事件本身的逻辑，"以理服人"，实现逻辑说服策略。情感资源实现情感说服目的，这是因为新闻语篇或多或少都添加了新闻作者和新闻人物的感情色彩，通过语篇中的情感资源建立渗透型态度韵律，感染读者，"以情动人"，促使读者接受语篇立场和观点，体现情感说服策略。

第五，在"一带一路"对外新闻语篇中，介入策略和话语空间都受到该语类结构与语域特征的影响。而这归根到底是由语篇交际目的决定的，即为对外宣传"一带一路"倡议营造出客观中立、平等协商、和谐包容的对话空间，赢得读者尊重和信任，影响读者阅读立场，建立作者与读者的评价同盟，引导读者接受作者观点："五通"发展旨在造福"一带一路"沿线的国家和民众，本着共建共享、互惠互利的精神，中国和沿线国家不遗余力推动"五通"发展，合作成果显著，未来发展潜力巨大。

第六,中欧"一带一路"对外新闻更注重人品说服的修辞策略,较大篇幅运用判断资源和主导型韵律模式报道中国和欧洲各国领导人的外交言论,体现他们高瞻远瞩的政治觉悟和一心为民的治国理念;中亚"一带一路"对外新闻更注重逻辑说服的修辞策略,较大篇幅运用鉴赏资源和增强型韵律模式报道中国和亚洲各国的合作领域、方式和层次,体现区域合作的巨大潜力和重大意义;中非"一带一路"对外新闻更注重情感说服的修辞策略,较大篇幅运用情感资源和渗透型韵律模式报道非洲各国加入"一带一路"建设的强烈愿望,以及对该倡议的赞赏和信任,强调该倡议在非洲大陆的历史文化背景,尤其是对非洲普通民众的意义,体现"一带一路"在非洲逐渐深入人心,建立了坚实的民意基础;中拉"一带一路"对外新闻更注重逻辑说服的修辞策略,较大篇幅运用鉴赏资源和增强型韵律模式报道中国与拉美各国合作项目的潜力和意义,体现"一带一路"建设和拉美地区的发展需求高度契合。

二、研究不足和建议

虽然本研究扩展了"一带一路"对外新闻语篇的研究维度,揭示了各种介入和态度话语资源在该类新闻语篇中的分布规律,话语韵律的人际意义、交际目的和修辞功能,但是也存在局限性。

第一,"一带一路"对外新闻语篇数量庞大,种类繁多,本研究无法穷尽所有相关语料,只从中国一带一路网、*China Daily* 和 Xinhua News Agency 上选取一部分英文对外新闻进行分析,有一定片面性,所以后期研究可以选取更多新闻报道,建立更大语料库,使得此类新闻语篇的话语策略研究结果更精确,更有代表性。

第二,有关"一带一路"对外新闻语篇介入和态度资源的判断和解读,目前没有电脑软件可以自动筛选识别,而是研究者依据评价理论介入和态度系统的分类标准,结合语篇语境进行判断,因此带有一定主观性,所以后期研究可以与更多研究者讨论鉴别介入和态度资源种类,并结合语境要素分析语篇评价策略的修辞功能和人际意义,最大限度减少个人主观判断,使得研究结果更客观准确。

参考文献

[1] Alexanne D. "It is hard to mesh all this": Invoking attitude, persona and argument organization. Functional Linguistics, 2016, 4(1): 1-26.

[2] Aristotle. The Art of Rhetoric. tr. H. C. Lawson-Tancred. London: Penguin Books, 1991.

[3] Bakhtin M. The Dialogic Imagination. Austin: University of Texas Press, 1981.

[4] Bakhtin M. Problems of Dostoevsky's Poetics. Minneapolis: University of Minnesota Press, 1984.

[5] Bell A. The Language of News Media. Oxford: Blackwell Publishers, 1991.

[6] Bell A. & Garrett P. Approaches to Media Discourse. Oxford: Blackwell Publisher, 1998.

[7] Blair H. Lectures on Rhetoric and Belles Lettres. Austin: Palala Press, 2015.

[8] Campbell G. The Philosophy of Rhetoric. Carbondale: Southern Illinois University Press, 1963.

[9] Corbett E P J. Classical Rhetoric for the Modern

Student. New York:Oxford University Press, 1999.

[10] Eggins S. An Introducing to Systemic Functional Linguistics. New York: Continuum International Publishing Group Ltd. , 2004.

[11] Fairclough N. Discourse and Social Change. Cambridge: Polity Press, 1992.

[12] Fairclough N. Media Discourse. London: Edward Arnold, 1995.

[13] Halliday M A K. Language as Social Semiotic. London: Edward Arnold, 1978.

[14] Halliday M A K. An Introduction to Functional Grammar. 3rd edition. London: Edward Arnold, 2004.

[15] Hoey M. Lexical Priming: A New Theory of Words and Language. London: Routledge, 2005.

[16] Hunston S. & Thompson G. Evaluation in Text: Authorial Stance and the Construction of Discourse. Oxford: Oxford University Press, 2000.

[17] Khoo C S G. , Nourbakhsh A. & Na J C. Sentiment Analysis of Online News Text: A Case Study of Appraisal Theory. Online Information Review, 2012, 8(6): 858-878.

[18] Korenek P. Sentiment Analysis on Microblog Utilizing Appraisal Theory. World Wide Web-Internet & Web Information Systems, 2014, 10(4):847-867.

[19] Kristeva J. Word, Dialogue and Novel. New York: Columbia University press, 1986.

[20] Kristeva J. The Kristeva Readers. Oxford: Basil Blackwell,1986.

[21] Lee H S. Evaluative Stances in Persuasive Essays by Undergraduate Students: Focusing on Appreciation Resources. Text & Talk, 2015, 6(1): 49-76.

[22] MacDougall C D. Interpretive Reporting. New York: Macmillan Publishing, 1982.

[23] Martin J R. English Text: System and Structure. Philadelphia:John Benjamins, 1992.

[24] Martin J R. Beyond Exchange: Appraisal Systems inEnglish. Hunston S & Thompson G//Evaluation in Text: Authorial Stance and the Construction of Discourse. Oxford: Oxford University Press, 2000.

[25] Martin J R. & Rose D. Working with Discourse: Meaning beyond the Clause. New York: Continuum, 2002.

[26] Martin J R. & White P R R. The Language of Evaluation: Appraisal in English. London: Palgrave Macmillan, 2005.

[27] Mencher M. Melvin Mencher's News Reporting and Writing. New York: McGraw-Hill Education, 2010.

[28] Mindich D T Z. Just the Facts: How "Objectivity" Came to Define American Journalism. New

York and London: NYU Press, 1998.

[29] Ngo T. & Unsworth L. Reworking the Appraisal Framework in ESL Research: Refining Attitude Resources. Functional Linguistics, 2015, 8(1): 1-24.

[30] Pagano A. Advances in Written Text Analysis. London: Routledge, 1994.

[31] Roux R. & Valladares M. Mexican Secondary School Teachers' Linguistic Expression of Attitude towards the National English Program in Basic Education. International Journal of Applied Linguistics & English Literature, 2015, 7(5): 620-625.

[32] Schudson M. The Power of News. New York: Harvard University Press, 1982.

[33] Schwartz J. Aristotle and the Future of Rhetoric. College Composition & Communication, 1966, 8 (5): 210-216.

[34] Sinclair J. The Search for Units of Meaning. TEXTUS, 1996, 9(1): 75-106.

[35] Thompson G. Introducing Functional Grammar. Beijing: Foreign Language Teaching and Research Press, 2000.

[36] Van Dijk T. News as Discourse. Hillsdale, New Jersey: Lawrence Erlbaum Associates, 1988.

[37] Van Dijk T. Racism and the Press. London:

Routledge，1991.

[38] Van Leeuwen T. Generic Strategies in Press Journalism. Australian Review of Applied Linguistics,1987, 80(4):199-220.

[39] Voloshinov V N. Marxism and the Philosophy of Language, Bakhtinian Thought—An Introductory Reader. London:Routledge, 1995.

[40] White P R R. Death, Disruption and the Moral Order: The Narrative Impulse in Mass-Media "Hard News" Reporting. Christie F & Martin J R//Genres and Institution: Social Processes in the Workplace and School. London: Cassell, 1997.

[41] White P R R. Telling Media Tales: The News Story as Rhetoric. New South Wales: University of Sydney,1998.

[42] White P R R. Media objectivity and the rhetoric of news story structure. Ventola E//Discourse and Community. Doing Functional Linguistics. Tubingen: Gunter Narr Verlag, 2000.

[43] White P R R. Appraisal: The Language of Evaluation and Stance. Verschueren J. , Ostman J. , Blommaert J. & Bulcaen C//The Handbook of Pragmatics. Amsterdam/Philadelphia: John Benjamins Publishing Co, 2002.

［44］White P R R. Beyond modality and hedging：A Dialogic View of the Language of Intersubjective Stance. Text-Special Edition on Appraisal，2003，26(4)：259-284.

［45］安珊珊，梁馨月. 美国新闻报道框架建构下的"中国形象"——美国主流媒体"一带一路"峰会新闻报道框架解析. 哈尔滨工业大学学报(社会科学版)，2018，64(2)：82-88.

［46］白文昌. 亚里士多德"说服三原则"对课堂教学的启示. 西南林业大学学报，2018，30(1)：47-50.

［47］陈令君，赵闯. 新闻语篇中的"中国梦"——评价理论态度视域下的话语分析. 天津外国语大学学报，2016，86(4)：34-39.

［48］陈梅，文军. 评价理论态度系统视阈下的白居易诗歌英译研究. 外语教学，2013，56(4)：99-104.

［49］程朝阳. 法庭调解语言中的修辞技艺探析——以亚里士多德的古典修辞学思想为线索. 北方法学，2014，36(4)：118-129.

［50］程果. 国际舆论形式下的"一带一路"建设宣传. 新闻研究导刊，2015，46(11)：256-262.

［51］程微. 态度韵律的整体性研究. 外语学刊，2010，46(3)：68-73.

［52］狄艳华，柳锦. 评价理论介入视角下的反恐语篇否认资源分析. 东北师范大学学报(哲学社会科学版)，2016，81(3)：125-130.

[53] 董希骁. 从新闻标题看罗马尼亚媒体对"一带一路"的态度. 中国外语, 2018, 32(3): 52-58.

[54] 董媛媛, 田晨. 对外新闻传播研究. 中国出版, 2017, 98(18): 49-52.

[55] 范红. 报刊新闻语篇及其宏观、微观结构. 清华大学学报(哲学社会科学版), 2002, 17(S1): 34-38.

[56] 樊明明. 话语权力在两种文化中的结构与功能——中西古典修辞学中说服三要素比较. 外语学刊, 1999, 16(3): 28-32.

[57] 高山, 刘智信. 关于新闻结构的构想. 齐齐哈尔社会科学, 1999, 38(6): 60-66.

[58] 葛琴. 基于态度系统的汉英政治新闻语篇对比分析. 外国语言文学, 2015, 33(2): 86-91.

[59] 管淑红. 意识流小说《达洛卫夫人》的态度系统研究. 华东交通大学学报, 2011, 38(3): 98-103.

[60] 韩颖. 格林童话的教育功能探析——以评价意义为视角. 外语与外语教学, 2014, 46(3): 5-10.

[61] 何伟, 高然. 新西兰媒体之中国"一带一路"倡议表征研究——以《新西兰先驱报》为例. 中国外语, 2018, 32(3): 46-51.

[62] 胡美馨, 黄银菊. 《中国日报》和《纽约日报》态度资源运用对比研究——以美军在利比亚军事行动报道为例. 外语研究, 2014, 42(4): 24-30.

[63] 华进. 窗口·微内容·标题轴: 网络新闻结构新

解. 青年记者，2013，58(2)：62-63.

[64] 蒋国东，陈许. 对外新闻中的"一带一路"——评价理论介入系统下的话语分析. 外语研究，2017，32(5)：6-9.

[65] 蒋平，王琳琳.《背影》及其英译的态度意义比较. 当代外语研究，2010，28(6)：23-27.

[66] 蒋婷. 态度系统视阈下仲裁员调解话语的人际意义分析. 现代外语，2016，33(2)：188-197.

[67] 江晓红. 语篇对话视角的介入分析. 深圳大学学报，2011，78(2)：110-113.

[68] 江潇潇. 斯里兰卡"一带一路"相关报道态度资源研究. 解放军外国语学院学报，2018，42(6)：42-48.

[69] 蒋岳春. 对比手法的使用与"一带一路"的表征——以《华盛顿邮报》为例. 中国外语，2018，40(3)：59-65.

[70] 鞠玉梅. 英汉学术论文语篇中的元话语研究——从亚里士多德修辞学的角度. 外语研究，2013，28(3)：23-29.

[71] 鞠玉梅.《论语》英译文语篇评价系统之判断资源的修辞功能. 当代修辞学，2016，38(5)：37-48.

[72] 李基安. 情态与介入. 外国语，2008，16(4)：60-63.

[73] 李静涵，韩晋. 寻找原本的"法律修辞学"：一个学说史的视角. 研究生法学，2017，40(3)：17-26.

[74] 李君，张德禄. 电视新闻访谈介入特征的韵律性模式探索. 外语教学，2010，31(4)：6-10.

[75] 李锡春. 广义新闻结构探析. 记者摇篮，2009，85 (9)：4-5.

[76] 李晓雪，黄滔. 美国主流报纸对中国阅兵报道态度差异研究——基于评价理论视角. 广东外语外贸大学学报，2017，40(2)：110-118.

[77] 李鑫. 评价理论中的态度系统与政治外宣文本翻译研究. 语文学刊，2016，30(5)：106-109.

[78] 李雪威，赵连雪. 日本主流报刊媒体的"一带一路"报道变化分析——以《日本经济新闻》《读卖新闻》为例. 现代日本经济，2018，221(5)：39-51.

[79] 李战子. 评价理论在：话语分析中的应用和问题. 外语研究，2004，20(5)：1-6.

[80] 廖杨标. 对外经济新闻报道框架分析——基于《人民日报》海外版"一带一路"报道的内容分析. 传播与版权，2015，46(11)：171-172.

[81] 林美珍. 农业语篇的介入资源分析：基于评价理论的视角. 福建农林大学学报（哲学社会科学版），2011，14 (3)：91-94.

[82] 刘世铸. 态度的结构潜势. 北京：中国社会科学出版社，2007.

[83] 刘婷婷，徐加新. 英汉政治社论语篇介入资源对比研究——评价理论视域下的新闻语篇分析. 外语与翻译，2018，98(3)：45-51.

[84] 刘亚猛. 西方修辞学史. 北京：外语教学与研究出

版社，2008.

[85] 刘再起，王蔓莉."一带一路"战略与中国参与全球治理研究——以话语权和话语体系为视角. 学习与实践，2016，78(4)：68-74.

[86] 马伟林.人际功能的拓展——评价系统述评.南京社会科学，2007，38(6)：142-146.

[87] 毛伟.新华社在拉美地区传播"一带一路"倡议的现状与效果.国际传播，2018，65(3)：48-55.

[88] 聂薇. 话语修辞与英国国家形象构建——以英国外长第 70 届联大演讲为例. 外国语文，2017，44(3)：67-72.

[89] 聂薇.从功能语言学看英国主流媒体对"一带一路"倡议的态度变化.解放军外国语学院学报，2018，41(6)：34-41.

[90] 宁留甫.跨国设施联通：历史启示与现实风险.宁夏社会科学，2016，196(3)：90-95.

[91] 潘小珏.介入资源与法庭辩论中说服的实现.修辞学习，2008，146(2)：50-55.

[92] 彭宣维. 从评价理论反观亚里士多德有关思想. 山东外语教学，2012，45(1)：16-20.

[93] 钱建伟，Rob Law. 基于评价理论介入系统的积极话语分析——以关于中国游客的评论性新闻报道为例. 广西社会科学，2016，252(6)：167-171.

[94] 乔榛."一带一路"建设的政策沟通功能.学术交流，2018，287(2)：106-111.

[95] 阮宗泽. 中国需要构建怎样的周边. 国际问题研究,2014,36(2):11-26.

[96] 单理扬. 媒体话语的隐喻叙事研究——以美国主流报刊对"一带一路"倡议的隐喻塑造为例. 山东外语教学,2017,52(4):17-26.

[97] 尚必武.《灿烂千阳》中的态度系统及其运作:以评价理论为研究视角. 山东外语教学,2008,56(4):18-23.

[98] 尚智慧. 新闻语篇的对话性及其对意识形态的构建. 外语与外语教学,2011,56(4):43-47.

[99] 邵斌,蔡颖莹,余晓燕. 西方媒体视野中"一带一路"形象的语料库探析. 当代外语研究,2018,28(4):40-47.

[100] 邵颖. 马来西亚官方媒体对"一带一路"的认知. 中国外语,2018,32(3):72-77.

[101] 史安斌,盛阳. "一带一路"背景下我国对外传播的创新路径. 新闻与写作,2017,68(8):10-13.

[102] 施光. 法庭审判话语的态度系统研究. 现代外语,2016,32(1):52-63.

[103] 施光. 刑事判决书的态度系统研究. 外语与外语教学,2017,42(6):81-88.

[104] 司显柱,庞玉厚. 评价理论、态度系统与语篇翻译. 中国外语,2018,30(1):96-102.

[105] 孙力. "一带一路"愿景下政策沟通的着力点. 新疆师范大学学报(哲学社会科学版),2016,37(3):33-39.

[106] 孙有中,江璐. 澳大利亚主流媒体中的"一带一

路".新闻学与传播学，2017，249(4)：37-44.

[107]谭姗燕.报刊新闻结构形式的认知语言学解读.山西农业大学学报，2005，46(3)：304-306.

[108]唐丽萍.英语学术书评的评价策略——从对话视角的介入分析.外语学刊，2005，125(4)：1-7.

[109]唐丽萍.两种评价韵律的演进、对视与反思.外语研究，2017，38(6)：38-42.

[110]唐青叶，史晓云.国外媒体"一带一路"话语表征对比研究——一项基于报刊语料库的话语政治分析.外语教学，2018，48(5)：31-35.

[111]田华静.身份建构的态度资源——以《悉尼先锋晨报》的一篇新闻报道为例.当代外语研究，2015，28(6)：5-12.

[112]汪波.韩国三大报刊对"一带一路"倡议的认知分析.解放军外国语学院学报，2018，41(6)：49-55.

[113]王军.国外传统韵律研究的最新进展及思考.外国语，2013，34(6)：18-26.

[114]王秋彬，崔庭赫.关于加强"一带一路"国际话语权构建的思考.公共外交季刊，2015，26(4)：60-66.

[115]王妍.修辞、真理与德性：古典反讽的多维解读.新疆大学学报，2019，41(3)：98-104.

[116]王义桅."一带一路"的国际话语权探析.探索，2016，30(2)：46-54.

[117]王振华.评价系统及其运作—系统功能语言学的

新发展. 外国语,2001,22(6):13-20.

[118] 王振华. 介入:言语互动中的一种评价视角. 开封:河南大学,2003.

[119] 王志远."一带一路"愿景下贸易畅通的新视点. 新疆师范大学学报(哲学社会科学版),2016,37(3):47-54.

[120] 王宗炎. 字斟句酌品标题——若干失误评点. 媒介批评,2009,68(25):49-50.

[121] 夏春平. 中新社"一带一路"报道解析. 对外传播,2015,36(4):29-31.

[122] 辛斌,吴玲莉. 中美媒体有关"一带一路"倡议报道中的介入资源分析. 外语研究,2018,40(6):1-7.

[123] 杨洸,郭中实. 新闻内容、理解与记忆:解读争议性事件报道的心智模型. 新闻与传播研究,2016,64(11):35-40.

[124] 袁传有. 警察讯问语言的人际意义——评价理论之"介入系统"视角. 现代外语,2008,31(2):141-149.

[125] 周凯. 全球化背景下"一带一路"建设的对外传播. 对外传播,2015,78(3):18-20.

[126] 赵福利. 英语电视新闻导语的语步结构分析. 外语教学与研究,2001,46(3):99-103.

[127] 赵雅莹,郭继荣,车向前. 评价理论视角下英国对"一带一路"态度研究. 情报杂志,2016,78(35):37-41.

[128] 张德禄. 功能文体学. 济南:山东教育出版社,1998.

[129] 张虹. 南非媒体视角的"一带一路". 中国外语，2018，68(3)：66-71.

[130] 张莉，陆洪磊. 影响国际议题报道的全球化和本土化因素的再思考—基于"一带一路"报道的比较研究. 新闻学与传播学，2018，267(10)：45-62.

[131] 张少奇. 批评话语分析视角下中美媒体关于中国"一带一路"新闻报道的对比研究. 北京：外交学院，2017.

[132] 张莹. 基于语料库的语义韵20年研究概述. 外语研究，2012，24(6)：23-28.

[133] 张允，朱卉. 基于百度指数下多媒体平台"一带一路"报道的政策性新闻受众关注度分析. 新闻知识，2015，86(6)：25-27.

[134] 郑华，李婧. 美国媒体建构下的中国"一带一路"战略构想——基于《纽约时报》和《华盛顿邮报》的相关报道分析. 上海对外经贸大学学报，2016，23(1)：87-96.

[135] 钟馨. 英国全国性报纸中"一带一路"话语的意义建构研究——基于语料库批评话语分析法. 新闻学与传播学，2018，264(7)：61-69.

[136] 朱桂生，黄建滨. 美国主流媒体视野中的中国"一带一路"战略——基于《华盛顿邮报》相关报道的批评性话语分析. 新闻界，2016，202(17)：58-64.

附　录

来自"中国一带一路网"的新闻语料题目

1. B&R memorandum opens up new prospects for China-New Zealand cooperation（31 March 2017）

2. Nepal set to promote pashmina products in China via Belt and Road platform（27 March 2017）

3. Cambodia to focus on infrastructure development at B&R forum（7 April 2017）

4. B&R Initiative opens up new prospects for China-Jordan cooperation（14 April 2017）

5. China signs education agreement for the Belt and Road（12 April 2017）

6. China，Russia to promote integration of B&R Initiative and Eurasian Economic Union（14 April 2017）

7. The Belt and Road Forum for International Cooperation to be held on May 14 and 15（18 April 2017）

8. Belt and Road forum agenda set（19 April 2017）

9. B&R offers new platform for Bulgaria-China cooperation（21 April 2017）

10. China，Belarus to cooperate on security issues under B&R Initiative (26 April 2017)

11. Belt and Road promotes growth of Cambodia's special economic zone (28 April 2017)

12. Belt and Road Initiative on agenda for Danish PM's China visit (2 May 2017)

13. Education，tourism highlight China-ASEAN cooperation (2 May 2017)

14. Belt and Road Initiative provides new growth point for the world: Belarusian President (8 May 2017)

15. Belt and Road Initiative beneficial for regional prosperity: IMF official (8 May 2017)

16. Kenyan president says B&R forum to revitalize Africa-China ties (12 May 2017)

17. China，Poland highlight cooperation under Belt and Road Initiative (13 May 2017)

18. China，Turkey to strengthen cooperation under B&R Initiative (14May 2017)

19. Belt and Road Portal included on list of BRF deliverables (16 May 2017)

20. New pact to boost tourism under Belt and Road Initiative (24 May 2017)

21. Cooperation grows between China，B&R countries (25 May 2017)

22. Belt and Road Initiative opens window of opportunity for Nepal (25 May 2017)

23. Cross-Straits fair highlights Belt and Road Initiative (26 May 2017)

24. SCO members boost connectivity under B&R Initiative (8 June 2017)

25. Xi, Putin meet on bilateral ties, SCO development (9 June 2017)

26. B&R Initiative enhance trade, investment in SCO countries(12 June 2017)

27. Xi's Kazakhstan trip carries on "Silk Road Spirit", charts new chapter (12 June 2017

28. B&R Initiative to boost tourism development in all participating countries (13 June 2017)

29. Nepal, China to deepen cooperation in literature under B&R Initiative (14 June 2017)

30. China, Kuwait to deepen cooperation under Belt and Road (14 June 2017)

31. Belt & Road Initiative to open new stage of cooperation (16 June 2017)

32. B&R Initiative highlighted at think-tank dialogue on China-US economic ties (16 June 2017)

33. Chinese vice-premier stresses building of Belt and Road (19 June 2017)

34. China-CEEC "16 + 1 cooperation" mechanism fruitful (20 June 2017)

35. China, Russia vow to enhance fiscal, financial cooperation (20 June 2017)

36. Belt and Road Initiative promoting new energy development (21 June 2017)

37. Belt and Road Initiative calls for talent with less commonly taught language skills (22 June 2017)

38. China opens wider to foreign investors with shortened FTZ negative list (23 June 2017)

39. Chinese, Ukrainian university chiefs discuss cooperation in higher education (26 June 2017)

40. Chinese express delivery firms tap Belt and Road markets (27 June 2017)

41. Xi's trip to inject positive energy into global economy (28 June 2017)

42. Belt and Road Initiative highlights China's strong sense of responsibility (28 June 2017)

43. B&R Initiative spurs more international industrial hubs (28 June 2017)

44. Heilongjiang plays significant role in Belt and Road Initiative (30 June 2017)

45. Belt and Road forum to be held in Paris (3 July 2017)

46. Xi greets AU leaders on summit（4 July 2017）

47. ICBC Standard Bank releases Belt and Road analysis（5 July 2017）

48. Xi's Moscow visit witnesses stronger China-Russia ties（5 July 2017）

49. China，Russia set up RMB investment fund（6 July 2017）

50. China eyes more cooperation with France under Belt and Road（6 July 2017）

51. China to offer solutions to economic globalization at G20 Hamburg summit（6 July 2017）

52. Xinjiang Week of 2017 Astana Expo excels（7 July 2017）

53. China expects G20 Hamburg summit to reach consensus on free trade：official（7 July 2017）

54. Xi says China welcomes Hamburg to participate in B&R Initiative（7 July 2017）

55. Xi，Abe meet on ties（10 July 2017）

56. G20 consensus highlights cooperation as major trend in global governance（11 July 2017）

57. Guangdong province keen to forge closer EU ties（11 July 2017）

58. First phase of Thai-Chinese high speed rail project approved by Thai cabinet（12 July 2017）

59. Henan to connect Silk Roads on land and sea (12 July 2017)

60. Belt and Road Initiative boosts Chinese-Polish ties (13 July 2017)

61. BFA Bangkok Conference: B&R gives impetus to interconnected development (13 July 2017)

62. China eyes more cooperation with Equatorial Guinea on B&R construction (14 July 2017)

63. China, Portugal to step up cooperation under B&R Initiative (14 July 2017)

64. B&R Initiative brings initial benefit for CEE countries (17 July 2017)

65. Belt, Road lay development path for China's vocational colleges (17 July 2017)

66. Heilongjiang-Russia trade ties blossom (18 July 2017)

67. Belt and Road is catalyst for rail (18 July 2017)

68. 1116+1 mechanism achieves fruitful results under B&R Initiative (19 July 2017)

69. Belt and Road Initiative complementary to 2030 Agenda for Sustainable Development (19 July 2017)

70. Sri Lanka Economic Summit 2017 to discuss Belt and Road Initiative (19 July 2017)

71. New rail connection links Czech Republic with

China's Yiwu (20 July 2017)

72. CPEC to help Pakistan ease power shortages, improve energy mix (20 July 2017)

73. China, Kazakhstan deepen energy cooperation (20 July 2017)

74. China vows increased cooperation with Tunisia on Belt and Road (21 July 2017)

75. Ambassador: China and Turkmenistan cooperate under B&R Initiative (21 July 2017)

76. Euro-Asia Economic Forum to be held in Xi'an (24 July 2017)

77. Chinese firms create over 28,000 jobs in Ethiopia over past five years (24 July 2017)

78. Latin America eyes opportunities in Belt and Road Initiative (24 July 2017)

79. International sinologists discuss Chinese culture in Beijing (25 July 2017)

80. B&R Initiative plays key role in Sino-Philippine ties (26 July 2017)

81. B&R Initiative expands China-Africa agri-cooperation (28 July 2017)

82. Small enterprises to benefit in Belt and Road markets (1 August 2017)

83. B&R Initiative brings ASEAN into golden era of

development (4 August 2017)

84. China, ASEAN agree to build higher level of strategic partnership (7 August 2017)

85. Belt and Road Initiative prompts Inner Mongolia's opening up (8 August 2017)

86. Ministry of Commerce: further promote Belt and Road construction (10 August 2017)

87. Belt and Road Initiative guides SMEs abroad (14 August 2017)

88. Belt and Road Initiative boosts yuan's internationalization (15 August 2017)

89. Belt and Road Initiative calls for intellectual support (17 August 2017)

90. Director-General leads WHO delegation to the Belt and Road Forum for Health Cooperation (17 August 2017)

91. Belt and Road countries to enhance health cooperation: communiqué (21 August 2017)

92. Belt and Road Initiative to strengthen China-Kuwait ties—Chinese envoy (22 August 2017)

93. B&R attracts capital, logistics enterprises to west China (24 August 2017)

94. B&R is a great contribution by China and Chinese people to the world, expert (29 August 2017)

95. China's VAT reform helps expand cooperation in

Belt and Road Initiative (30 August 2017)

96. BRICS eyes new opportunities in B&R Initiative (31 August 2017)

97. Nepal has high hopes from China's Belt and Road Initiative: Deputy PM (1 September 2017)

98. China, Brazil agree to further advance comprehensive strategic partnership (4 September 2017)

99. BRICS' synergy with Belt and Road Initiative (7 September 2017)

100. Chinese enterprises advised to pay heed to culture, tax issues in overseas M&A under B&R (8 September 2017)

101. Private enterprises important to Belt and Road projects (11 September 2017)

102. B&R Initiative to benefit Arctic Ocean economic circle: expert (14 September 2017)

103. China, Croatia could enhance ties under Belt and Road Initiative: ambassador (15 September 2017)

104. Officials call for closer ties between China, Black Sea under Belt and Road Initiative (19 September 2017)

105. China, Ukraine pledge to strengthen cooperation under Belt and Road Initiative (20 September 2017)

106. China, Cambodia agree to strengthen bilateral relations (20 September 2017)

107. China's B2B trade with Belt and Road countries booms (21 September 2017)

108. Chinese-Italian panel discusses cultural exchange opportunities (25 September 2017)

109. China，Serbia to deepen information technology cooperation (26 September 2017)

110. China to set up Belt and Road commercial court (28 September 2017)

111. Foreign banks increase renminbi exchanges on Belt and Road Initiative (30 September 2017)

112. China promotes benefit-sharing world through partnerships worldwide (3 October 2017)

113. Belt and Road building cultural bridges (12 October 2017)

114. B&R Initiative to make world "much richer"：Serbian president (16 October 2017)

115. Chinese environmental companies tap Belt and Road markets (17 October 2017)

116. Joint work team to deepen cooperation for China-Europe cargo train services (18 October 2017)

117. Cooperation in Eurasia beefs up under Belt and Road Initiative (19 October 2017)

118. Shenzhen looks to reap Belt and Road bonanza (20 October 2017)

119. Belt and Road Initiative gets FTZ boost (23 October 2017)

120. Tibet gains from Belt and Road Initiative (25 October 2017)

121. B&R Initiative markedly increases investment in Turkey (25 October 2017)

122. Transport most promising cooperation field between Poland, CEEC, China: Polish PM (26 October 2017)

123. Beijing offers Belt and Road scholarship (26 October 2017)

124. Foreign diplomats visit ancient Silk Road in southwest China (26 October 2017)

125. New high-speed railway to strengthen ties on Belt and Road (30 October 2017)

126. Shanghai Stock Exchange to deepen Belt and Road capital market cooperation (31 October 2017)

127. City of London opens talks with banks on Belt and Road investment (2 November 2017)

128. Belt and Road to shape global economy: report (3 November 2017)

129. Belt & Road Initiative reaches the Arctic (6 November 2017)

130. Egypt reaffirms support to China's B&R

Initiative, calling for more Chinese investment (7 November 2017)

131. Vietnam's first light rail results from Belt and Road Initiative (7 November 2017)

132. Financial agencies assume vital roles on Belt and Road (8 November 2017)

133. Belt and Road power projects help to solve Pakistan's electricity shortage (9 November 2017)

134. Belt and Road Initiative prompts Chinese standards to go abroad (9 November 2017)

135. Silk Road Fund, General Electric set up energy infrastructure investment platform (10 November 2017)

136. Chinese-European joint white paper set to strengthen int'l green bond market (13 November 2017)

137. Asian residents along Belt and Road get tangible benefits (14 November 2017)

138. Xi'an banking on SAR's status in B&R push (15 November 2017)

139. Experts explore China-Thailand cooperation opportunity under B&R (17 November 2017)

140. Belt and Road investment beckons (20 November 2017)

141. France sends Belt and Road Initiative study group to Xiamen (21 November 2017)

142. Belt and Road Initiative drives non-government cooperation (24 November 2017)

143. B&R is helping China's rise, says PwC (27 November 2017)

144. Incubation union for Belt and Road set up in Beijing (28 November 2017)

145. 21st Century Maritime Silk Road' Forum kicks off in Zhuhai, China (30 November 2017)

146. Belt and Road Vision opens new e-commerce window (6 December 2017)

147. Energy cooperation along B&R promising, experts (7 December 2017)

148. China, Greece vow to strengthen cooperation under Belt and Road (8 December 2017)

149. Sri Lanka joins China's Belt and Road with operations of Hambantota Port: PM (11 December 2017)

150. B&R could unleash new wave of globalization (12 December 2017)

151. Asset management firms see windfall from B&R Initiative (14 December 2017)

152. China-Africa industrial capacity cooperation expo opens in Kenya (14 December 2017)

153. China unveils outcomes of economic, financial dialogue with Britain (18 December 2017)

154. London, Hong Kong boost financial cooperation on Belt and Road Initiative (19 December 2017)

155. China, Italy to cooperate more on Belt and Road (20 December 2017)

156. Xi steers Chinese economy toward high-quality development (21 December 2017)

157. S. Korea seeks to play active role in Belt and Road Initiative (22 December 2017)

158. China-Thailand high-speed railway to be operational in early 2023: Thai minister (25 December 2017)

159. China's B&R Initiative to benefit Southeast Asian countries: Singaporean experts (25 December 2017)

160. Belt and Road Initiative gains traction in France (25 December 2017)

161. Belt and Road seen as best partnership tool (25 December 2017)

162. Belt and Road reaches out to more peoples, lands (25 December 2017)

163. Made in China' Christmas products sweep the globe (27 December 2017)

164. China, Sri Lanka's joint development in Hambantota turns from vision to reality in 2017 (28 December 2017)

165. Xi calls for more efforts in major-country diplomacy with Chinese characteristics (29 December 2017)

166. China-Bangladesh friendship, cooperation continue to expand in 2017 (29 December 2017)

167. China's B&R fund helps Afghan, Mongolian children with heart diseases (2 January 2018)

168. Xi says China ready to promote mutual trust, cooperation with Russia in 2018 (2 January 2018)

169. China, Laos sign agreement on Lancang-Mekong cooperation fund (3 January 2018)

170. Cargo trains make record trips between Yangtze River Delta, Europe (3 January 2018)

171. Belt and Road miracles in number in 2017 (4 January 2018)

172. Xiamen to issue certificate of origin to Georgia (4 January 2018)

173. Digital platform provides support for B&R Initiative, expert (4 January 2018)

174. Chinese premier's visit to Cambodia enhances bilateral ties, Lancang-Mekong cooperation: ambassador (8 January 2018)

175. Global survey shows China's B&R initiative receives more world recognition (8 January 2018)

176. Macron vows active participation in Belt and Road

Initiative (9 January 2018)

177. China, Cambodia expand cooperation under Belt & Road, Rectangular Strategy (10 January 2018)

178. Lancang-Mekong Cooperation puts people first, brings benefits to locals (10 January 2018)

179. China-Vietnam border business brings delicious cooperation (11 January 2018)

180. China releases meteorological development plan under Belt & Road (11 January 2018)

181. Chinese and Cambodian firms sign 34 trade agreements (12 January 2018)

182. China welcomes EU gesture on Belt and Road Initiative (12 January 2018)

183. Chengdu launches Belt and Road scholarship programs to promote cultural exchange (17January 2018)

184. Jordan, China ink deal to boost aviation cooperation (17 January 2018)

185. UN official urges LatAm to make most of China's Belt and Road Initiative (22 January 2018)

186. Belt&Road Initiative brings opportunities to countries involved: US experts (18 January 2018)

187. Chinese FM ends Africa visit, confident in closer China-Africa ties (18 January 2018)

188. China-EU Tourism Year opens with official

ceremony in Venice (22 January 2018)

189. Construction of China-UAE trade center starts in east China (22 January 2018)

190. China-LAC cooperation to level up along "Belt and Road": FM (22 January 2018)

191. Chinese firms' non-financial direct investment in B&R countries in 2017 totaled 14.36 bln USD (22 January 2018)

192. Chinese president calls for concerted efforts with Latin America on B&R Initiative (23 January 2018)

193. CPEC opens job opportunities for unemployed Pakistanis (23 January 2018)

194. HKSAR, Belarus grant mutual visa-free access (26 January 2018)

195. China publishes Arctic policy, eyeing vision of ' Polar Silk Road' (29 January 2018)

196. China, Britain expect more results from Belt and Road Initiative cooperation: expert (30 January 2018)

197. China pledges to work for early conclusion of RCEP (31 January 2018)

198. Chinese, British banks sign deal on Belt and Road cooperation (2 February 2018)

199. Xi meets May, calling for better Sino-British ties in new era (2 February 2018)

200. Xi，Putin exchange congratulations on election win in phone talks（20 March 2018）

来自 *China Daily* 和 Xinhua News Agency 的新闻语料题目

201. Xi's Eurasia trip boosts Belt and Road（Xinhua News Agency 12 May 2015）

202. China，Kazakhstan agree to integrate growth strategies（Xinhua News Agency 27 June 2015）

203. Xi proposes closer China-Turkey business cooperation（Xinhua News Agency 31 July 2015）

204. Xi calls on China，US to enhance local-level cooperation（Xinhua News Agency 23 September 2015）

205. Xi calls for closer Asia-Pacific cooperation for common prosperity（Xinhua News Agency 19 November 2015）

206. China's EBRD membership a boost to Belt and Road Initiative：PBOC（Xinhua News Agency 15 December 2015）

207. China，Iran address thirst for growth（*China Daily* 24 January 2016）

208. Xi urges fostering sense of community of common destiny with Czech Republic（Xinhua News Agency 30 March 2016）

209. China，Switzerland forge innovative strategic partnership（Xinhua News Agency 9 April 2016）

210. China, Kazakhstan pledge to align development strategies (Xinhua News Agency 24 June 2016)

211. Belt and Road Initiative links China's development with that of Serbia, Poland, Uzbekistan (Xinhua News Agency 26 June 2016)

212. President Xi calls for cooperation with Greece (*China Daily* 5 July 2016)

213. Officials call for closer IP ties among Belt and Road nations (*China Daily* 27 July 2016)

214. Xi calls for advancing Belt and Road Initiative (Xinhua News Agency 18 August 2016)

215. Xi vows to cement all-round strategic partnership with Malaysia (Xinhua News Agency 4 November 2016)

216. President Xi calls for aligning development strategies of China, Italy (Xinhua News Agency 17 November 2016)

217. Xi, Putin meet on Asia-Pacific free trade, China-Russia ties (Xinhua News Agency 20 November 2016)

218. China, Peru agree to promote better, faster growth of ties (Xinhua News Agency 22 November 2016)

219. Xi, Kuczynski pledge stronger China-LatAm cultural exchanges (Xinhua News Agency 23 November 2016)

220. China, Chile lift ties to comprehensive strategic

partnership (Xinhua News Agency 23 November 2016)

221. Xi eyes closer China-Spain cooperation (Xinhua News Agency 25 November 2016)

222. China, Vietnam agree to manage differences on South China Sea (Xinhua News Agency 14 January 2017)

223. Chinese, Sri Lankan presidents exchange congratulations on anniversary of diplomatic ties (Xinhua News Agency 8 February 2017)

224. New Zealand keen to work with China on free trade, globalization (*China Daily* 8 February 2017)

225. China, Israel announce innovative comprehensive partnership (Xinhua News Agency 22 March 2017)

226. China welcomes Madagascar to join B&R construction (Xinhua News Agency 28 March 2017)

227. China, Nepal to cooperate more on Belt and Road (Xinhua News Agency 28 March 2017)

228. Xi's visit to draw blueprint for China-Finland partnership (Xinhua News Agency 4 April 2017)

229. China, Finland agree to advance ties, deepen cooperation (Xinhua News Agency 5 April 2017)

230. China, UAE agree to advance strategic partnership (Xinhua News Agency 3 May 2017)

231. China calls for cooperation with Denmark under B&R initiative (Xinhua News Agency 5 May 2017)

232. Belt and Road Initiative provides new growth point for the world: Belarusian President (*China Daily* 7 May 2017)

233. Chinese, Vietnamese presidents hold talks on ties (Xinhua News Agency 11 May 2017)

234. Xi urges broader cooperation with Uzbekistan in building B&R (Xinhua News Agency 12 May 2017)

235. Xi urges broader cooperation with Czech Republic (Xinhua News Agency 12 May 2017)

236. Xi proposes advancing China-Ethiopia ties (Xinhua News Agency 12 May 2017)

237. Xi urges upgrading of free trade agreement with Switzerland (Xinhua News Agency 13 May 2017)

238. Xi calls for strengthened strategic coordination between China, Kazakhstan (Xinhua News Agency 14 May 2017)

239. Xi says China, Russia play role of "ballast stone" in world peace, stability (Xinhua News Agency 14 May 2017)

240. Xi suggests aligning B&R initiative with European investment plan (Xinhua News Agency 16 May 2017)

241. China, Argentina pledge to strengthen bilateral ties (Xinhua News Agency 17 May 2017)

242. China highly appreciates Vietnam's support,

participation in B&R Initiative: official (Xinhua News Agency 22 May 2017)

243. Chinese FM pledges further cooperation with African countries on Belt and Road (Xinhua News Agency 23 May 2017)

244. Putin says to advance Russia-China cooperation under B&R Initiative (Xinhua News Agency 2 June 2017)

245. Spain to boost cooperation with China under Belt & Road Initiative (Xinhua News Agency 5 June 2017)

246. President Xi eyes bigger role for California in China-US cooperation (Xinhua News Agency 6 June 2017)

247. Xi's Kazakhstan visit to boost bilateral cooperation, chart course for SCO development (Xinhua News Agency 7 June 2017)

248. China and Afghanistan should deepen Belt and Road cooperation, Xi says (*China Daily* 8 June 2017)

249. Xi's Kazakhstan trip carries on "Silk Road Spirit", charts new chapter (Xinhua News Agency 11 June 2017)

250. China and Panama establish diplomatic relations (Xinhua News Agency 13 June 2017)

251. Luxembourg expected to play active role in developing China-EU ties (Xinhua News Agency 15 June 2017)

252. Belt & Road Initiative to open new stage of

cooperation: Putin (Xinhua News Agency 16 June 2017)

253. China, Russia vow to enhance fiscal, financial cooperation (Xinhua News Agency 19 June 2017)

254. China, Ghana pledge to have more win-win cooperation (Xinhua News Agency 22 June 2017)

255. Nepal, China hail smooth, healthy development of bilateral ties (Xinhua News Agency 22 June 2017)

256. Chinese, Ukrainian university chiefs discuss cooperation in higher education (Xinhua News Agency 24 June 2017)

257. Chinese president meets Finnish PM on strengthening cooperation Road (Xinhua News Agency 27 June 2017)

258. President Xi says CICA meeting to contribute to regional peace (Xinhua News Agency 28 June 2017)

259. Xi greets AU leaders on summit (*China Daily* 4 July2017)

260. Xi's Moscow visit witnesses stronger China-Russia ties (Xinhua News Agency 5 July 2017)

261. China, Germany pledge to take bilateral ties to higher levels (Xinhua News Agency 6 July 2017)

262. Xi urges mutual understanding with Singapore on core interests, major concerns (Xinhua News Agency 7 July 2017)

263. Xi says China welcomes Hamburg to participate in B&R Initiative (Xinhua News Agency 7 July 2017)

264. Xi eyes more stable, rapid development of ties with Britain (Xinhua News Agency 10 July 2017)

265. Kuwait, China to boost ties in all possible fields: Kuwaiti envoy (Xinhua News Agency 10 July 2017)

266. Belt and Road Initiative boosts Chinese-Polish ties (Xinhua News Agency 13 July 2017)

267. China, Poland urged to seize opportunity of B&R Initiative for closer cooperation (Xinhua News Agency 17 July 2017)

268. Palestine to discuss cooperation with China on B&R Initiative (Xinhua News Agency 17 July 2017)

269. China, Czech Republic eye increased cooperation under B&R Initiative (Xinhua News Agency 19 July 2017)

270. China plays important role in promoting stability, development of Africa: Tunisian FM (Xinhua News Agency 21 July 2017)

271. Xi's diplomacy promotes inclusiveness (*China Daily* 24 July 2017)

272. B&R Initiative plays key role in Sino-Philippine ties (Xinhua News Agency 26 July 2017)

273. Chinese FM eyes new prospect for China-Indonesia ties (Xinhua News Agency 27 July 2017)

274. Xi calls for cooperation on fighting desertification (Xinhua News Agency 31 July 2017)

275. China and Brazil to upgrade ties (Xinhua News Agency 2 August 2017)

276. Chinese FM highlights mutual trust, cooperation with Singapore, Cambodia (Xinhua News Agency 7 August 2017)

277. China, Africa to strengthen cooperation, innovation on renewable energy (Xinhua News Agency 8 August 2017)

278. China, Japan ruling parties hold talks on improving ties (Xinhua News Agency 10 August 2017)

279. Sri Lankan president thanks China for strong assistance, support (Xinhua News Agency 11 August 2017)

280. China, Pakistan vow to further deepen bilateral pragmatic cooperation (Xinhua News Agency 14 August 2017)

281. Pakistani president meets Chinese vice premier on deepening Pakistan-China friendship (Xinhua News Agency 15 August 2017)

282. China, Nepal vow to further promote pragmatic cooperation (Xinhua News Agency 16 August 2017)

283. Belt and Road Initiative calls for intellectual support (Xinhua News Agency 17 August 2017)

284. China, Laos to enhance cooperation in information, culture, tourism (Xinhua News Agency 18 August 2017)

285. China, Saudi Arabia agree to strengthen economic ties (Xinhua News Agency 21 August 2017)

286. Belt and Road Initiative to strengthen China-Kuwait ties—Chinese envoy (Xinhua News Agency 22 August 2017)

287. Pakistan eager to proceed with Belt and Road projects (*China Daily* 23 August 2017)

288. Belt and Road set to boost development in Mideast, Africa (Xinhua News Agency 24 August 2017)

289. Vice premier meets Sudanese PM, pledging pragmatic cooperation (Xinhua News Agency 28 August 2017)

290. B&R is a great contribution by China and Chinese people to the world, expert (Xinhua News Agency 29 August 2017)

291. China, ASEAN set new model for regional cooperation, expert (Xinhua News Agency 31 August 2017)

292. China, Tajikistan agree to forge comprehensive strategic partnership (Xinhua News Agency 1 September 2017)

293. China, Brazil agree to further advance

comprehensive strategic partnership (Xinhua News Agency 4 September 2017)

294. Xi, Putin agree to enhance strategic coordination (Xinhua News Agency 4 September 2017)

295. China to enhance cooperation with Thailand: Xi (Xinhua News Agency 5 September 2017)

296. China to advance comprehensive strategic partnership with Egypt (Xinhua News Agency 6 September 2017)

297. China, Uzbekistan agree to strengthen cooperation (Xinhua News Agency 11 September 2017)

298. China, Brunei to boost ties (Xinhua News Agency 14 September 2017)

299. China, Ukraine pledge to strengthen cooperation under Belt and Road Initiative (Xinhua News Agency 20 September 2017)

300. Xi meets Singaporean PM on advancing ties (Xinhua News Agency 21 September 2017)

301. Xi, British PM discuss bilateral ties over phone (Xinhua News Agency 26 September 2017)

302. Istanbul's governor vows efforts to promote Turkey's ties with China (Xinhua News Agency 27 September 2017)

303. China, Serbia to deepen information technology

cooperation (Xinhua News Agency 28 September 2017)

304. China vows to work closely with ASEAN to build community with shared future (Xinhua News Agency 24 October 2017)

305. Xi stresses commitment to good China-Russia relations (Xinhua News Agency 2 November 2017)

306. Vietnam, China vow to join hands to realize common prosperity (Xinhua News Agency 6 November 2017)

307. Xi, Duterte meet on strengthening China-Philippines ties (Xinhua News Agency 13 November 2017)

308. Xi sheds new light on Asia-Pacific cooperation (Xinhua News Agency 13 November 2017)

309. Xi calls for more China-Laos cooperation in public welfare (Xinhua News Agency 15 November 2017)

310. Sino-African friendship groups reaffirm cooperation's role (*China Daily* 20 November 2017)

311. China proposes building China-Myanmar economic corridor to boost cooperation (Xinhua News Agency 20 November 2017)

312. Myanmar president says willing to work with China to expedite Belt and Road development (Xinhua News Agency 21 November 2017)

313. Chinese FM calls for jointly building new type of

Asia-Europe partnership （Xinhua News Agency 21 November 2017)

314. Xi calls on NGOs along Silk Road to enhance cooperation (Xinhua News Agency 21 November 2017)

315. China，Djibouti agree to establish strategic partnership (Xinhua News Agency 24 November 2017)

316. Chinese ambassador says China，Russia to strengthen digital economy cooperation （Xinhua News Agency 28 November 2017)

317. Chinese premier pledges to expand win-win cooperation with Serbia，Slovenia，BiH （Xinhua News Agency 29 November 2017)

318. Chinese premier pledges joint efforts with Russia to promote regional cooperation (Xinhua News Agency 30 November 2017)

319. China to promote building a community of shared future for the world：Xi (Xinhua News Agency 1 December 2017)

320. Xi welcomes countries to ride fast train of internet，digital economy （Xinhua News Agency 4 December 2017)

321. President Xi meets with visiting ROK President Moon (Xinhua News Agency 15 December 2017)

322. China，Italy to cooperate more on Belt and Road

（Xinhua News Agency 20 December 2017）

323. China to improve people-to-people exchanges with foreign countries （Xinhua News Agency 22 December 2017）

324. Chinese foreign minister pledges better diplomacy for China, world development （Xinhua News Agency 26 December 2017）

325. Xi says China ready to promote mutual trust, cooperation with Russia in 2018 （Xinhua News Agency 2 January 2018）

326. Premier Li's visit to Cambodia to boost Lancang-Mekong cooperation （Xinhua News Agency 5 January 2018）

327. Xi, Macron celebrate joint progress （*China Daily* 10 January 2018）

328. China will maintain cooperation with Laos: premier （Xinhua News Agency 10 January 2018）

329. China welcomes EU gesture on Belt and Road Initiative （Xinhua News Agency 12 January 2018）

330. Chinese president calls for concerted efforts with Latin America on B&R Initiative （Xinhua News Agency 23 January 2018）

331. China, Britain expect more results from Belt and Road Initiative cooperation: expert （Xinhua News Agency 30 January 2018）

332. Xi meets May, calling for better Sino-British ties

in new era (Xinhua News Agency 2 February 2018)

333. Chinese president meets Dutch king, calls for closer cooperation on B&R construction (Xinhua News Agency 8 February 2018)

334. China, Indonesia to cooperate under B&R initiative (Xinhua News Agency 11 February 2018)

335. China, Tonga agree to promote strategic partnership (Xinhua News Agency 2 March 2018)

336. China to strengthen financing support for Belt and Road Initiative (Xinhua News Agency 9 March 2018)

337. Xi calls for exemplary win-win cooperation with Germany (Xinhua News Agency 19 March 2018)

338. China, Cameroon agree to further advance relationship (Xinhua News Agency 23 March 2018)

339. China, Namibia agree to establish comprehensive strategic partnership of cooperation (Xinhua News Agency 30 March 2018)

340. Xi stresses need to improve global governance during meeting with UN chief (Xinhua News Agency 9 April 2018)

341. China, Netherlands agree to exploit advantages of complementarities(Xinhua News Agency 13 April 2018)

342. China, Britain agree to further promote golden era of bilateral ties (Xinhua News Agency 20 April 2018)

343. Xi says he's looking forward to planning China-Russia ties with Putin in new era (Xinhua News Agency 24 April 2018)

344. Xi expects meeting with Modi to open new chapter in China-India ties (Xinhua News Agency 28 April 2018)

345. Chinese premier calls for concrete measures to reinforce China-Indonesia ties (Xinhua News Agency 8 May 2018)

346. Xi calls for integration of development strategies between China, Trinidad and Tobago (Xinhua News Agency 16 May 2018)

347. China, Netherlands willing to strengthen cooperation on B&R (Xinhua News Agency 22 May 2018)

348. Xi meets Merkel, calls for higher-level China-Germany ties (Xinhua News Agency 25 May 2018)

349. China, EU vow to deepen strategic cooperation, safeguard multilateralism (Xinhua News Agency 4 June 2018)

350. China, Kazakhstan agree to work together for respective national rejuvenation (Xinhua News Agency 8 June 2018)

351. China vows to boost imports for balanced trade and consumption upgrading (Xinhua News Agency 14 June 2018)

352. China, Britain seek deeper insurance cooperation under Belt and Road Initiative (Xinhua News Agency 19 June 2018)

353. Xi says China to enhance mutually beneficial cooperation with Nepal (Xinhua News Agency 21 June 2018)

354. China, Kuwait agree to establish strategic partnership (Xinhua News Agency 10 July 2018)

355. Germany's Commerzbank partners with ICBC to support Belt & Road projects (Xinhua News Agency 20 July 2018)

356. Xi meets Mauritian PM on bilateral ties (Xinhua News Agency 30 July 2018)

357. China, Britain hold strategic dialogue, agree to jointly maintain multilaterism (Xinhua News Agency 31 July 2018)

358. Xi meets Malaysian PM, calling for better ties in new era (Xinhua News Agency 21 August 2018)

359. Xi to deliver keynote speech at FOCAC: FM (Xinhua News Agency 23 August 2018)

360. Ministers hold meeting to expand China-Britain cooperation (Xinhua News Agency 27 August 2018)

361. Belt and Road construction brings no debt trap for relevant countries: Chinese official (Xinhua News Agency

28 August 2018)

362. Xi encourages youth to build Belt, Road (*China Daily* 30 August 2018)

363. Xi meets Gabonese president (Xinhua News Agency 3 September 2018)

364. The CAR, at heart of Africa, ready to join Belt and Road Initiative—president (Xinhua News Agency 3 September 2018)

365. Economic Forum participants discuss Belt and Road Initiative in Poland (Xinhua News Agency 7 September 2018)

366. Xi calls for strengthening cooperation in Northeast Asia for regional peace, prosperity (Xinhua News Agency 13 September 2018)

367. China, Suriname vow to deepen cooperation under BRI framework (Xinhua News Agency 25 September 2018)

368. China, Angola agree to promote ties as presidents meet in Beijing (Xinhua News Agency 10 October 2018)

369. China to boost ties with Tajikistan to new levels: Premier Li (Xinhua News Agency 15 October 2018)

370. China, Belgium to strengthen cooperation (Xinhua News Agency 18 October 2018)

371. Xi meets Japanese Prime Minister, urging effort to cherish positive momentum in ties (Xinhua News Agency

29 October 2018)

372. China-Pakistan joint declaration highlights vision of economic corridor, trade, investment (*China Daily* 6 November 2018)

373. China to further strengthen scientific cooperation with B&R countries (Xinhua News Agency 7 November 2018)

374. Xi holds talks with Cuban president to advance ties (Xinhua News Agency 9 November 2018)

375. China, Spain agree to advance ties during Xi's visit (Xinhua News Agency 29 November 2018)

376. Xi demonstrates China's critical, constructive role in G20 (Xinhua News Agency 3 December 2018)

377. China, Portugal pledge to jointly push forward construction of Belt and Road (Xinhua News Agency 6 December 2018)

378. China, Germany agree to further intensify bilateral ties (Xinhua News Agency 12 December 2018)

379. Xi welcomes Ecuador to help build Belt, Road (*China Daily* 13 December 2018)

380. China, Egypt agree to promote pragmatic cooperation in all fields (Xinhua News Agency 18 January 2019)

381. Chinese vice president calls for closer innovation

cooperation with Switzerland (Xinhua News Agency 23 January 2019)

382. China, France ready to steadily boost ties: Chinese FM (Xinhua News Agency 25 January 2019)

383. Chinese, Italian FMs pledge closer bilateral cooperation (Xinhua News Agency 28 January 2019)

384. China, Pakistan to enhance cooperation on Belt and Road Initiative (Xinhua News Agency 18 February 2019)

385. China, Kuwait vow to deepen pragmatic cooperation on B&R Initiative (Xinhua News Agency 19 February 2019)

386. China, Saudi Arabia agree to expand cooperation (Xinhua News Agency 25 February 2019)

387. China, Laos agree to promote people-to-people communication (Xinhua News Agency 25 February 2019)

388. China-UK cooperation on Belt and Road Initiative to be promoted through 3 phases (Xinhua News Agency 11 March 2019)

389. China, Sri Lanka jointly build green Belt and Road projects (Xinhua News Agency 15 March 2019)

390. Xi, Conte hold talks on elevating China-Italy ties into new era (Xinhua News Agency 25 March 2019)

391. Xi, Macron agree to forge more solid, stable,

vibrant China-France partnership（Xinhua News Agency 26 March 2019）

392. Xi meets European leaders on advancing ties，global governance（Xinhua News Agency 28 March 2019）

393. China's BRI provides development opportunity for Ecuador（Xinhua News Agency 10 April 2019）

394. China says Belt，Road will not get involved in territorial disputes（*China Daily* 16 April 2019）

395. BRI cooperation helps Cambodia diversify economy，strengthen resilience（Xinhua News Agency 22 April 2019）

396. Ethiopia expects to sign major power project deal with China during BRF（Xinhua News Agency 24 April 2019）

397. China-proposed BRI boosts LatAm development（Xinhua News Agency 26 April 2019）

398. Xi underlines high-quality development of Belt and Road（Xinhua News Agency 27 April 2019）

399. China，Kyrgyzstan vow to strengthen practical cooperation under BRI（Xinhua News Agency 23 May 2019）

400. Xi holds talks with Nigerien President，vowing to boost ties（Xinhua News Agency 29 May 2019）

索　引